PENGUIN BOOKS

DEVOTIONS

Born in a small town in Ohio, Mary Oliver published her first book of poetry in 1963 at the age of twenty-eight. Over the course of her long career, she received numerous awards. Her fourth book, *American Primitive*, won the Pulitzer Prize for Poetry in 1984. She led workshops and held residencies at various colleges and universities, including Bennington College, where she held the Catharine Osgood Foster Chair for Distinguished Teaching. She died in 2019.

Select Titles Also by Mary Oliver

Devotions

THE SELECTED POEMS OF MARY OLIVER

Mary Oliver

PENGUIN BOOKS

PENGUIN BOOKS
An imprint of Penguin Random House LLC
penguinrandomhouse.com

First published in the United States of America by Penguin Press,
an imprint of Penguin Random House LLC, 2019
Published in Penguin Books 2020

ISBN 9780399563263 (paperback)

THE LIBRARY OF CONGRESS HAS CATALOGED THE HARDCOVER EDITION AS FOLLOWS:
Names: Oliver, Mary, 1935– author.
Title: Devotions : the selected poems of Mary Oliver / Mary Oliver.
Description: New York : Penguin Press, 2017.
Identifiers: LCCN 2017025254 (print) | LCCN 2017027796 (ebook) | ISBN
9780399563256 (ebook) | ISBN 9780399563249 (hardcover)
Subjects: | BISAC: Poetry / General. | Poetry / American / General.
Classification: LCC PS3565.L5 (ebook) | LCC PS3565.L5 A6 2017 (print) |
DDC
811/.54—dc23
LC record available at https://lccn.loc.gov/2017025254

Printed in the United States of America
11th Printing

BOOK DESIGN BY AMANDA DEWEY

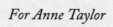

For Anne Taylor

CONTENTS

from *Felicity*
2015

from *Blue Horses*
2014

FROM *Dog Songs*
2013

FROM *A Thousand Mornings*
2012

FROM *Swan*

2010

FROM *Evidence*

2009

FROM *The Truro Bear and Other Adventures*
2008

FROM *Red Bird*
2008

FROM *Thirst*
2006

FROM *New and Selected Poems: Volume Two* 2005

FROM *Blue Iris*
2004

FROM *Why I Wake Early*
2004

FROM *Long Life*
2004

FROM *Owls and Other Fantasies*
2003

FROM *What Do We Know?*
2002

FROM *The Leaf and the Cloud*
2000

FROM *West Wind*
1997

FROM *White Pine*
1994

FROM *New and Selected Poems:*
Volume One 1992

FROM *House of Light*
1990

FROM *Dream Work*
1986

FROM *American Primitive*
1983

FROM *Three Rivers Poetry Journal* 1980
AND "THREE POEMS FOR JAMES WRIGHT" 1982

FROM *Twelve Moons*
1979

FROM *The River Styx, Ohio*
1972

FROM *No Voyage and Other Poems*
1963 and 1965

DEVOTIONS

FROM

Felicity

2015

I WAKE CLOSE TO MORNING

Why do people keep asking to see
      God's identity papers
when the darkness opening into morning
      is more than enough?
Certainly any god might turn away in disgust.
Think of Sheba approaching
      the kingdom of Solomon.
Do you think she had to ask,
      "Is this the place?"

THIS MORNING

This morning the redbirds' eggs
have hatched and already the chicks
are chirping for food. They don't
know where it's coming from, they
just keep shouting, "More! More!"
As to anything else, they haven't
had a single thought. Their eyes
haven't yet opened, they know nothing
about the sky that's waiting. Or
the thousands, the millions of trees.
They don't even know they have wings.

And just like that, like a simple
neighborhood event, a miracle is
taking place.

THE WORLD I LIVE IN

I have refused to live
locked in the orderly house of
　　reasons and proofs.
The world I live in and believe in
is wider than that. And anyway,
　　what's wrong with *Maybe*?

You wouldn't believe what once or
twice I have seen. I'll just
　　tell you this:
only if there are angels in your head will you
　　ever, possibly, see one.

WHISTLING SWANS

Do you bow your head when you pray or do you look
   up into that blue space?
Take your choice, prayers fly from all directions.
And don't worry about what language you use,
God no doubt understands them all.
Even when the swans are flying north and making
such a ruckus of noise, God is surely listening
   and understanding.
Rumi said, There is no proof of the soul.
But isn't the return of spring and how it
springs up in our hearts a pretty good hint?
Yes, I know, God's silence never breaks, but is
   that really a problem?
There are thousands of voices, after all.
And furthermore, don't you imagine (I just suggest it)
that the swans know about as much as we do about
   the whole business?
So listen to them and watch them, singing as they fly.
Take from it what you can.

STORAGE

When I moved from one house to another
there were many things I had no room
for. What does one do? I rented a storage
space. And filled it. Years passed.
Occasionally I went there and looked in,
but nothing happened, not a single
twinge of the heart.
As I grew older the things I cared
about grew fewer, but were more
important. So one day I undid the lock
and called the trash man. He took
everything.
I felt like the little donkey when
his burden is finally lifted. Things!
Burn them, burn them! Make a beautiful
fire! More room in your heart for love,
for the trees! For the birds who own
nothing—the reason they can fly.

FOR TOM SHAW S.S.J.E. (1945–2014)

Where has this cold come from?
"It comes from the death of your friend."

Will I always, from now on, be this cold?
"No, it will diminish. But always
      it will be with you."

What is the reason for it?
"Wasn't your friendship always as beautiful
  as a flame?"

I KNOW SOMEONE

I know someone who kisses the way
a flower opens, but more rapidly.
Flowers are sweet. They have
short, beatific lives. They offer
much pleasure. There is
nothing in the world that can be said
against them.
Sad, isn't it, that all they can kiss
is the air.

Yes, yes! We are the lucky ones.

THAT LITTLE BEAST

That pretty little beast, a poem,
    has a mind of its own.
Sometimes I want it to crave apples
    but it wants red meat.
Sometimes I want to walk peacefully
    on the shore
and it wants to take off all its clothes
    and dive in.

Sometimes I want to use small words
    and make them important
and it starts shouting the dictionary,
    the opportunities.

Sometimes I want to sum up and give thanks,
    putting things in order
and it starts dancing around the room
    on its four furry legs, laughing
    and calling me outrageous.

But sometimes, when I'm thinking about you,
    and no doubt smiling,
it sits down quietly, one paw under its chin,
    and just listens.

THE POND

August of another summer, and once again
I am drinking the sun
and the lilies again are spread across the water.
I know now what they want is to touch each other.
I have not been here for many years
during which time I kept living my life.
Like the heron, who can only croak, who wishes he
    could sing,
I wish I could sing.
A little thanks from every throat would be appropriate.
This is how it has been, and this is how it is:
All my life I have been able to feel happiness,
except whatever was not happiness,
which I also remember.
Each of us wears a shadow.
But just now it is summer again
and I am watching the lilies bow to each other,
then slide on the wind and the tug of desire,
close, close to one another.
Soon now, I'll turn and start for home.
And who knows, maybe I'll be singing.

I HAVE JUST SAID

I have just said
   something
ridiculous to you
   and in response,

your glorious laughter.
   These are the days
the sun
   is swimming back

to the east
   and the light on the water
gleams
   as never, it seems, before.

I can't remember
   every spring,
I can't remember
   everything—

so many years!
   Are the morning kisses
the sweetest
   or the evenings

or the inbetweens?
   All I know

is that "thank you" should appear
somewhere.

So, just in case
I can't find
the perfect place—
"Thank you, thank you."

THE GIFT

Be still, my soul, and steadfast.
Earth and heaven both are still watching
though time is draining from the clock
and your walk, that was confident and quick,
has become slow.

So, be slow if you must, but let
the heart still play its true part.
Love still as once you loved, deeply
and without patience. Let God and the world
know you are grateful.
That the gift has been given.

FROM

Blue Horses

2014

AFTER READING LUCRETIUS,
I GO TO THE POND

The slippery green frog
that went to his death
in the heron's pink throat
was my small brother,

and the heron
with the white plumes
like a crown on his head
who is washing now his great sword-beak
in the shining pond
is my tall thin brother.

My heart dresses in black
and dances.

I DON'T WANT TO BE DEMURE
OR RESPECTABLE

I don't want to be demure or respectable.
I was that way, asleep, for years.
That way, you forget too many important things.
How the little stones, even if you can't hear them,
    are singing.
How the river can't wait to get to the ocean and
    the sky, it's been there before.
What traveling is that!
It is a joy to imagine such distances.
I could skip sleep for the next hundred years.
There is a fire in the lashes of my eyes.
It doesn't matter where I am, it could be a small room.
The glimmer of gold Böhme saw on the kitchen pot
    was missed by everyone else in the house.

Maybe the fire in my lashes is a reflection of that.
Why do I have so many thoughts, they are driving me
    crazy.
Why am I always going anywhere, instead of
    somewhere?
Listen to me or not, it hardly matters.
I'm not trying to be wise, that would be foolish.
I'm just chattering.

STEBBIN'S GULCH

by the randomness
of the way
the rocks tumbled
ages ago

the water pours
it pours
it pours
ever along the slant

of downgrade
dashing its silver thumbs
against the rocks
or pausing to carve

a sudden curled space
where the flashing fish
splash or drowse
while the kingfisher overhead

rattles and stares
and so it continues for miles
this bolt of light,
its only industry

to descend
and to be beautiful
while it does so;
as for purpose

. . .

there is none,
it is simply
one of those gorgeous things
that was made

to do what it does perfectly
and to last,
as almost nothing does,
almost forever.

FRANZ MARC'S BLUE HORSES

I step into the painting of the four blue horses.
I am not even surprised that I can do this.

One of the horses walks toward me.
His blue nose noses me lightly. I put my arm
over his blue mane, not holding on, just
    commingling.
He allows me my pleasure.
Franz Marc died a young man, shrapnel in his brain.
I would rather die than try to explain to the blue horses
    what war is.
They would either faint in horror, or simply
    find it impossible to believe.
I do not know how to thank you, Franz Marc.
Maybe our world will grow kinder eventually.
Maybe the desire to make something beautiful
    is the piece of God that is inside each of us.
Now all four horses have come closer,
    are bending their faces toward me
        as if they have secrets to tell.
I don't expect them to speak, and they don't.
If being so beautiful isn't enough, what
    could they possibly say?

ON MEDITATING, SORT OF

Meditation, so I've heard, is best accomplished
if you entertain a certain strict posture.
Frankly, I prefer just to lounge under a tree.
So why should I think I could ever be successful?

Some days I fall asleep, or land in that
even better place—half-asleep—where the world,
spring, summer, autumn, winter—
flies through my mind in its
hardy ascent and its uncompromising descent.

So I just lie like that, while distance and time
reveal their true attitudes: they never
heard of me, and never will, or ever need to.

Of course I wake up finally
thinking, how wonderful to be who I am,
made out of earth and water,
my own thoughts, my own fingerprints—
all that glorious, temporary stuff.

LONELINESS

I too have known loneliness.

I too have known what it is to feel

    misunderstood,

    rejected, and suddenly

not at all beautiful.

Oh, mother earth,

    your comfort is great, your arms never withhold.

It has saved my life to know this.

Your rivers flowing, your roses opening in the morning.

Oh, motions of tenderness!

DO STONES FEEL?

Do stones feel?
Do they love their life?
Or does their patience drown out everything else?

When I walk on the beach I gather a few
    white ones, dark ones, the multiple colors.
Don't worry, I say, I'll bring you back, and I do.

Is the tree as it rises delighted with its many
    branches,
each one like a poem?

Are the clouds glad to unburden their bundles of rain?

Most of the world says no, no, it's not possible.

I refuse to think to such a conclusion.
Too terrible it would be, to be wrong.

DRIFTING

I was enjoying everything: the rain, the path
    wherever it was taking me, the earth roots
    beginning to stir.
I didn't intend to start thinking about God,
    it just happened.
How God, or the gods, are invisible,
    quite understandable.
But holiness is visible, entirely.
It's wonderful to walk along like that,
    thought not the usual intention to reach an answer
    but merely drifting.
Like clouds that only seem weightless
    but of course are not.
Are really important.
I mean, terribly important.
Not decoration by any means.
By next week the violets will be blooming.
Anyway, this was my delicious walk in the rain.
What was it actually about?

Think about what it is that music is trying to say.
It was something like that.

BLUEBERRIES

I'm living in a warm place now, where
you can purchase fresh blueberries all
year long. Labor free. From various
countries in South America. They're
as sweet as any, and compared with the
berries I used to pick in the fields
outside of Provincetown, they're
enormous. But berries are berries. They
don't speak any language I can't
understand. Neither do I find ticks or
small spiders crawling among them. So,
generally speaking, I'm very satisfied.

There are limits, however. What they
don't have is the field. The field they
belonged to and through the years I
began to feel I belonged to. Well,
there's life, and then there's later.
Maybe it's myself that I miss. The
field, and the sparrow singing at the
edge of the woods. And the doe that one
morning came upon me unaware, all
tense and gorgeous. She stamped her hoof
as you would to any intruder: Then gave
me a long look, as if to say, Okay, you
stay in your patch, I'll stay in mine.
Which is what we did. Try packing that
up, South America.

THE VULTURE'S WINGS

The vulture's
wings are
black death
color but
the underwings
as sunlight
flushes into
the feathers
are bright
are swamped
with light.
Just something
explainable by
the sun's
angle yet
I keep
looking I
keep wondering
standing so
far below
these high
floating birds
could this
as most
things do
be offering
something for
us to
think about
seriously?

WHAT GORGEOUS THING

I do not know what gorgeous thing
the bluebird keeps saying,
his voice easing out of his throat,
beak, body into the pink air
of the early morning. I like it
whatever it is. Sometimes
it seems the only thing in the world
that is without dark thoughts.
Sometimes it seems the only thing
in the world that is without
questions that can't and probably
never will be answered, the
only thing that is entirely content
with the pink, then clear white
morning and, gratefully, says so.

FROM

Dog Songs

2013

THE STORM

Now through the white orchard my little dog
    romps, breaking the new snow
    with wild feet.
Running here running there, excited,
    hardly able to stop, he leaps, he spins
until the white snow is written upon
    in large, exuberant letters,
a long sentence, expressing
    the pleasures of the body in this world.

Oh, I could not have said it better
    myself.

PERCY (ONE)

Our new dog, named for the beloved poet,
ate a book which unfortunately we had
    left unguarded.
Fortunately it was the *Bhagavad Gita*,
of which many copies are available.
Every day now, as Percy grows
into the beauty of his life, we touch
his wild, curly head and say,

"Oh, wisest of little dogs."

LITTLE DOG'S RHAPSODY IN THE NIGHT
(PERCY THREE)

He puts his cheek against mine
and makes small, expressive sounds.
And when I'm awake, or awake enough

he turns upside down, his four paws
    in the air
and his eyes dark and fervent.

Tell me you love me, he says.

Tell me again.

Could there be a sweeter arrangement? Over and over
he gets to ask it.
I get to tell.

PERCY (NINE)

Your friend is coming I say
to Percy, and name a name

and he runs to the door, his
wide mouth in its laugh-shape,

and waves, since he has one, his tail.
Emerson, I am trying to live,

as you said we must, the examined life.
But there are days I wish

there was less in my head to examine,
not to speak of the busy heart. How

would it be to be Percy, I wonder, not
thinking, not weighing anything, just running forward.

BENJAMIN, WHO CAME FROM WHO KNOWS WHERE

What shall I do?
When I pick up the broom
   he leaves the room.
When I fuss with kindling he
   runs for the yard.
Then he's back, and we
   hug for a long time.
In his low-to-the-ground chest
   I can hear his heart slowing down.
Then I rub his shoulders and
   kiss his feet
and fondle his long hound ears.
   Benny, I say,
don't worry. I also know the way
   the old life haunts the new.

THE DOG HAS RUN OFF AGAIN

and I should start shouting his name
and clapping my hands,
but it has been raining all night
and the narrow creek has risen
is a tawny turbulence is rushing along
over the mossy stones
is surging forward
with a sweet loopy music
and therefore I don't want to entangle it
with my own voice
calling summoning
my little dog to hurry back
look the sunlight and the shadows are chasing each other
listen how the wind swirls and leaps and dives up and down
who am I to summon his hard and happy body
his four white feet that love to wheel and pedal
through the dark leaves
to come back to walk by my side, obedient.

BAZOUGEY

Where goes he now, that dark little dog
    who used to come down the road barking and shining?
He's gone now, from the world of particulars,
    the singular, the visible.

So, that deepest sting: sorrow. Still,
    is he gone from us entirely, or is he
a part of that other world, everywhere?

Come with me into the woods where spring is
    advancing, as it does, no matter what,
not being singular or particular, but one
    of the forever gifts, and certainly visible.

See how the violets are opening, and the leaves
    unfolding, the streams gleaming and the birds
    singing. What does it make you think of?
His shining curls, his honest eyes, his
    beautiful barking.

HER GRAVE

She would come back, dripping thick water, from the green bog.
She would fall at my feet, she would draw the black skin
from her gums, in a hideous and wonderful smile—
and I would rub my hands over her pricked ears and her
    cunning elbows,
and I would hug the barrel of her body, amazed at the unassuming
    perfect arch of her neck.

⸺∞⸺

It took four of us to carry her into the woods.
We did not think of music,
but, anyway, it began to rain
slowly.

⸺∞⸺

Her wolfish, invitational, half-pounce.

Her great and lordly satisfaction at having chased something.

My great and lordly satisfaction at her splash
of happiness as she barged
through the pitch pines swiping my face with her
wild, slightly mossy tongue.

⸺∞⸺

Does the hummingbird think he himself invented his crimson throat?
He is wiser than that, I think.

A dog lives fifteen years, if you're lucky.

. . .

Do the cranes crying out in the high clouds
think it is all their own music?

A dog comes to you and lives with you in your own house, but you
do not therefore own her, as you do not own the rain, or the
trees, or the laws which pertain to them.

Does the bear wandering in the autumn up the side of the hill
think all by herself she has imagined the refuge and the refreshment
of her long slumber?

A dog can never tell you what she knows from the
smells of the world, but you know, watching her, that you know
almost nothing.

Does the water snake with his backbone of diamonds think
the black tunnel on the bank of the pond is a palace
of his own making?

———⊗———

She roved ahead of me through the fields, yet would come back, or
wait for me, or be somewhere.

Now she is buried under the pines.

Nor will I argue it, or pray for anything but modesty, and
not to be angry.

. . .

Through the trees there is the sound of the wind, palavering.

The smell of the pine needles, what is it but a taste
of the infallible energies?

How strong was her dark body!
How apt is her grave place.

How beautiful is her unshakable sleep.

———∞∞———

Finally,
the slick mountains of love break
over us.

THE POETRY TEACHER

The university gave me a new, elegant
classroom to teach in. Only one thing,
they said. You can't bring your dog.
It's in my contract, I said. (I had
made sure of that.)

We bargained and I moved to an old
classroom in an old building. Propped
the door open. Kept a bowl of water
in the room. I could hear Ben among
other voices barking, howling in the
distance. Then they would all arrive—
Ben, his pals, maybe an unknown dog
or two, all of them thirsty and happy.
They drank, they flung themselves down
among the students. The students loved
it. They all wrote thirsty, happy poems.

THE FIRST TIME PERCY CAME BACK

The first time Percy came back
he was not sailing on a cloud.
He was loping along the sand as though
he had come a great way.
"Percy," I cried out, and reached to him—
      those white curls—
but he was unreachable. As music
is present yet you can't touch it.
"Yes, it's all different," he said.
"You're going to be very surprised."
But I wasn't thinking of that. I only
wanted to hold him. "Listen," he said,
"I miss that too.
And now you'll be telling stories
      of my coming back
and they won't be false, and they won't be true,
but they'll be real."
And then, as he used to, he said, "Let's go!"
And we walked down the beach together.

FROM

A Thousand Mornings

2012

I GO DOWN TO THE SHORE

I go down to the shore in the morning
and depending on the hour the waves
are rolling in or moving out,
and I say, oh, I am miserable,
what shall—
what should I do? And the sea says
in its lovely voice:
Excuse me, I have work to do.

I HAPPENED TO BE STANDING

I don't know where prayers go,
    or what they do.
Do cats pray, while they sleep
    half-asleep in the sun?
Does the opossum pray as it
    crosses the street?
The sunflowers? The old black oak
    growing older every year?
I know I can walk through the world,
    along the shore or under the trees,
with my mind filled with things
    of little importance, in full
self-attendance. A condition I can't really
    call being alive.
Is a prayer a gift, or a petition,
    or does it matter?
The sunflowers blaze, maybe that's their way.
Maybe the cats are sound asleep. Maybe not.

While I was thinking this I happened to be standing
just outside my door, with my notebook open,
which is the way I begin every morning.
Then a wren in the privet began to sing.

He was positively drenched in enthusiasm,
I don't know why. And yet, why not.

I wouldn't persuade you from whatever you believe
or whatever you don't. That's your business.
But I thought, of the wren's singing, what could this be
    if it isn't a prayer?
So I just listened, my pen in the air.

THREE THINGS TO REMEMBER

As long as you're dancing, you can
    break the rules.
Sometimes breaking the rules is just
    extending the rules.

Sometimes there are no rules.

LINES WRITTEN IN THE DAYS
OF GROWING DARKNESS

Every year we have been
witness to it: how the
world descends

into a rich mash, in order that
it may resume.
And therefore
who would cry out

to the petals on the ground
to stay,
knowing as we must,
how the vivacity of *what was* is married

to the vitality of *what will be?*
I don't say
it's easy, but
what else will do

if the love one claims to have for the world
be true?

So let us go on, cheerfully enough,
this and every crisping day,

though the sun be swinging east,
and the ponds be cold and black,
and the sweets of the year be doomed.

AN OLD STORY

Sleep comes its little while. Then I wake
in the valley of midnight or three a.m.
to the first fragrances of spring

which is coming, all by itself, no matter what.
My heart says, what you thought you have you do not have.
My body says, will this pounding ever stop?

My heart says: there, there, be a good student.
My body says: let me up and out, I want to fondle
those soft white flowers, open in the night.

THE INSTANT

Today
one small snake lay, looped and
solitary
in the high grass, it

swirled to look, didn't
like what it saw
and was gone
in two pulses

forward and with no sound at all, only
two taps, in disarray, from
that other shy one,
my heart.

TIDES

Every day the sea
   blue gray green lavender
pulls away leaving the harbor's
dark-cobbled undercoat

slick and rutted and worm-riddled, the gulls
walk there among old whalebones, the white
   spines of fish blink from the strandy stew
as the hours tick over; and then

far out the faint, sheer
   line turns, rustling over the slack,
the outer bars, over the green-furred flats, over
the clam beds, slippery logs,

barnacle-studded stones, dragging
the shining sheets forward, deepening,
   pushing, wreathing together
wave and seaweed, their piled curvatures

spilling over themselves, lapping
   blue gray green lavender, never
resting, not ever but fashioning shore,
continent, everything.

And here you may find me
on almost any morning
walking along the shore so
   light-footed so casual.

THE POET COMPARES HUMAN NATURE
TO THE OCEAN FROM WHICH WE CAME

The sea can do craziness, it can do smooth,
it can lie down like silk breathing
or toss havoc shoreward; it can give

gifts or withhold all; it can rise, ebb, froth
like an incoming frenzy of fountains, or it can
sweet-talk entirely. As I can too,

and so, no doubt, can you, and you.

LIFE STORY

When I lived under the black oaks
I felt I was made of leaves.
When I lived by Little Sister Pond,
I dreamed I was the feather of the blue heron
left on the shore;
I was the pond lily, my root delicate as an artery,
my face like a star,
my happiness brimming.
Later I was the footsteps that follow the sea.
I knew the tides, I knew the ingredients of the wrack.
I knew the eider, the red-throated loon
with his uplifted beak and his smart eye.
I felt I was the tip of the wave,
the pearl of water on the eider's glossy back.
No, there's no escaping, nor would I want to escape
this outgo, this foot-loosening, this solution
to gravity and a single shape.
Now I am here, later I will be there.
I will be that small cloud, staring down at the water,
the one that stalls, that lifts its white legs, that
    looks like a lamb.

VARANASI

Early in the morning we crossed the ghat,
where fires were still smoldering,
and gazed, with our Western minds, into the Ganges.
A woman was standing in the river up to her waist;
she was lifting handfuls of water and spilling it
over her body, slowly and many times,
as if until there came some moment
of inner satisfaction between her own life and the river's.
Then she dipped a vessel she had brought with her
and carried it filled with water back across the ghat,
no doubt to refresh some shrine near where she lives,
for this is the holy city of Shiva, maker
of the world, and this is his river.
I can't say much more, except that it all happened
in silence and peaceful simplicity, and something that felt
like the bliss of a certainty and a life lived
in accordance with that certainty.
I must remember this, I thought, as we fly back
to America.
Pray God I remember this.

FROM

Swan

2010

I WORRIED

I worried a lot. Will the garden grow, will the rivers
flow in the right direction, will the earth turn
as it was taught, and if not, how shall
I correct it?

Was I right, was I wrong, will I be forgiven,
can I do better?

Will I ever be able to sing, even the sparrows
can do it and I am, well,
hopeless.

Is my eyesight fading or am I just imagining it,
am I going to get rheumatism,
lockjaw, dementia?

Finally I saw that worrying had come to nothing.
And gave it up. And took my old body
and went out into the morning,
and sang.

I OWN A HOUSE

I own a house, small but comfortable. In it is a bed, a desk, a kitchen, a closet, a telephone. And so forth—you know how it is: things collect.

Outside the summer clouds are drifting by, all of them with vague and beautiful faces. And there are the pines that bush out spicy and ambitious, although they do not even know their names. And there is the mockingbird; over and over he rises from his thorn-tree and dances—he actually dances, in the air. And there are days I wish I owned nothing, like the grass.

DON'T HESITATE

If you suddenly and unexpectedly feel joy,
don't hesitate. Give in to it. There are plenty
of lives and whole towns destroyed or about
to be. We are not wise, and not very often
kind. And much can never be redeemed.
Still, life has some possibility left. Perhaps this
is its way of fighting back, that sometimes
something happens better than all the riches
or power in the world. It could be anything,
but very likely you notice it in the instant
when love begins. Anyway, that's often the
case. Anyway, whatever it is, don't be afraid
of its plenty. Joy is not made to be a crumb.

SWAN

Did you too see it, drifting, all night on the black river?
Did you see it in the morning, rising into the silvery air,
an armful of white blossoms,
a perfect commotion of silk and linen as it leaned
into the bondage of its wings: a snowbank, a bank of lilies,
biting the air with its black beak?
Did you hear it, fluting and whistling
a shrill dark music, like the rain pelting the trees,
  like a waterfall
knifing down the black ledges?
And did you see it, finally, just under the clouds—
a white cross streaming across the sky, its feet
like black leaves, its wings like the stretching light
  of the river?
And did you feel it, in your heart, how it pertained to everything?
And have you too finally figured out what beauty is for?
And have you changed your life?

PASSING THE UNWORKED FIELD

Queen Anne's lace
 is hardly
  prized but
all the same it isn't
  idle look
    how it
  stands straight on its
thin stems how it
  scrubs its white faces
  with the
rags of the sun how it
  makes all the
   loveliness
    it can.

HOW I GO TO THE WOODS

Ordinarily I go to the woods alone, with not a single friend, for they are all smilers and talkers and therefore unsuitable.

I don't really want to be witnessed talking to the catbirds or hugging the old black oak tree. I have my way of praying, as you no doubt have yours.

Besides, when I am alone I can become invisible. I can sit on the top of a dune as motionless as an uprise of weeds, until the foxes run by unconcerned. I can hear the almost unhearable sound of the roses singing.

—ᴏᴈᴏ—

If you have ever gone to the woods with me, I must love you very much.

ON THE BEACH

On the beach, at dawn:
four small stones clearly
hugging each other.

How many kinds of love
might there be in the world,
and how many formations might they make

and who am I ever
to imagine I could know
such a marvelous business?

When the sun broke
it poured willingly its light
over the stones

that did not move, not at all,
just as, to its always generous term,
it shed its light on me,

my own body that loves,
equally, to hug another body.

FROM

Evidence

2009

VIOLETS

Down by the rumbling creek and the tall trees—
    where I went truant from school three days a week
        and therefore broke the record—
there were violets as easy in their lives
    as anything you have ever seen
        or leaned down to intake the sweet breath of.
Later, when the necessary houses were built
    they were gone, and who would give significance
        to their absence.
Oh, violets, you did signify, and what shall take
    your place?

WE SHAKE WITH JOY

We shake with joy, we shake with grief.
What a time they have, these two
housed as they are in the same body.

IT WAS EARLY

It was early,
    which has always been my hour
        to begin looking
           at the world

and of course,
    even in the darkness,
        to begin
           listening into it,

especially
    under the pines
        where the owl lives
           and sometimes calls out

as I walk by,
    as he did
        on this morning.
           So many gifts!

What do they mean?
    In the marshes
        where the pink light
           was just arriving

the mink
    with his bristle tail
        was stalking
           the soft-eared mice,

. . .

and in the pines
    the cones were heavy,
        each one
            ordained to open.

Sometimes I need
    only to stand
        wherever I am
            to be blessed.

Little mink, let me watch you.
    Little mice, run and run.
        Dear pine cone, let me hold you
            as you open.

WITH THANKS TO THE FIELD SPARROW, WHOSE VOICE IS SO DELICATE AND HUMBLE

I do not live happily or comfortably
with the cleverness of our times.
The talk is all about computers,
the news is all about bombs and blood.
This morning, in the fresh field,
I came upon a hidden nest.
It held four warm, speckled eggs.
I touched them.
Then went away softly,
having felt something more wonderful
than all the electricity of New York City.

A LESSON FROM JAMES WRIGHT

If James Wright
could put in his book of poems
a blank page

dedicated to "the Horse David
Who Ate One of My Poems," I am ready
to follow him along

the sweet path he cut
through the dryness
and suggest that you sit now

very quietly
in some lovely wild place, and listen
to the silence.

And I say that this, too,
is a poem.

ALMOST A CONVERSATION

I have not really, not yet, talked with otter
    about his life.

He has so many teeth, he has trouble
    with vowels.

Wherefore our understanding
    is all body expression—

he swims like the sleekest fish,
he dives and exhales and lifts a trail of bubbles.
Little by little he trusts my eyes
and my curious body sitting on the shore.

Sometimes he comes close.
I admire his whiskers
and his dark fur which I would rather die than wear.

He has no words, still what he tells about his life
    is clear.
He does not own a computer.
He imagines the river will last forever.
He does not envy the dry house I live in.
He does not wonder who or what it is that I worship.
He wonders, morning after morning, that the river
is so cold and fresh and alive, and still
I don't jump in.

TO BEGIN WITH,
THE SWEET GRASS

1.

Will the hungry ox stand in the field and not eat
    of the sweet grass?
Will the owl bite off its own wings?
Will the lark forget to lift its body in the air or
    forget to sing?
Will the rivers run upstream?

Behold, I say—behold
the reliability and the finery and the teachings
    of this gritty earth gift.

2.

Eat bread and understand comfort.
Drink water, and understand delight.
Visit the garden where the scarlet trumpets
    are opening their bodies for the hummingbirds
who are drinking the sweetness, who are
    thrillingly gluttonous.

For one thing leads to another.
Soon you will notice how stones shine underfoot.
Eventually tides will be the only calendar you believe in.

And someone's face, whom you love, will be as a star
both intimate and ultimate,
and you will be both heart-shaken and respectful.

. . .

And you will hear the air itself, like a beloved, whisper:
oh, let me, for a while longer, enter the two
beautiful bodies of your lungs.

3.

The witchery of living
is my whole conversation
with you, my darlings.
All I can tell you is what I know.

Look, and look again.
This world is not just a little thrill for the eyes.

It's more than bones.
It's more than the delicate wrist with its personal pulse.
It's more than the beating of the single heart.
It's praising.
It's giving until the giving feels like receiving.
You have a life—just imagine that!
You have this day, and maybe another, and maybe
    still another.

4.

Someday I am going to ask my friend Paulus,
the dancer, the potter,

to make me a begging bowl
which I believe
my soul needs.

And if I come to you,
to the door of your comfortable house
with unwashed clothes and unclean fingernails,
will you put something into it?

I would like to take this chance.
I would like to give you this chance.

5.

We do one thing or another; we stay the same, or we
    change.
Congratulations, if
    you have changed.

6.

Let me ask you this.
Do you also think that beauty exists for some
    fabulous reason?

And, if you have not been enchanted by this adventure—
    your life—
what would do for you?

7.

What I loved in the beginning, I think, was mostly myself.
Never mind that I had to, since somebody had to.
That was many years ago.
Since then I have gone out from my confinements,
    though with difficulty.

I mean the ones that thought to rule my heart.
I cast them out, I put them on the mush pile.
They will be nourishment somehow (everything is nourishment
    somehow or another).

And I have become the child of the clouds, and of hope.
I have become the friend of the enemy, whoever that is.
I have become older and, cherishing what I have learned,
I have become younger.

And what do I risk to tell you this, which is all I know?
Love yourself. Then forget it. Then, love the world.

EVIDENCE

1.

Where do I live? If I had no address, as many people
do not, I could nevertheless say that I lived in the
same town as the lilies of the field, and the still
waters.

Spring, and all through the neighborhood now there are
strong men tending flowers.

Beauty without purpose is beauty without virtue. But
all beautiful things, inherently, have this function—
to excite the viewers toward sublime thought. Glory
to the world, that good teacher.

Among the swans there is none called the least, or
the greatest.

I believe in kindness. Also in mischief. Also in
singing, especially when singing is not necessarily
prescribed.

As for the body, it is solid and strong and curious
and full of detail; it wants to polish itself; it
wants to love another body; it is the only vessel in
the world that can hold, in a mix of power and
sweetness: words, song, gesture, passion, ideas,
ingenuity, devotion, merriment, vanity, and virtue.

Keep some room in your heart for the unimaginable.

2.

There are many ways to perish, or to flourish.

How old pain, for example, can stall us at the
threshold of function.

Memory: a golden bowl, or a basement without light.

For which reason the nightmare comes with its
painful story and says: *you need to know this.*

Some memories I would give anything to forget.
Others I would not give up upon the point of
death, they are the bright hawks of my life.

Still, friends, consider stone, that is without
the fret of gravity, and water that is without
anxiety.

And the pine trees that never forget their
recipe for renewal.

And the female wood duck who is looking this way
and that way for her children. And the snapping
turtle who is looking this way and that way also.
This is the world.

And consider, always, every day, the determination
of the grass to grow despite the unending obstacles.

3.

I ask you again: if you have not been enchanted by
this adventure—your life—what would do for
you?

And, where are you, with your ears bagged down
as if with packets of sand? Listen. We all
have much more listening to do. Tear the sand
away. And listen. The river is singing.

What blackboard could ever be invented that
could hold all the zeros of eternity?

Let me put it this way—if you disdain the
cobbler may I assume you walk barefoot?

Last week I met the so-called deranged man
who lives in the woods. He was walking with
great care, so as not to step on any small,
living thing.

For myself, I have walked in these woods for
more than forty years, and I am the only
thing, it seems, that is about to be used up.
Or, to be less extravagant, will, in the
foreseeable future, be used up.

. . .

First, though, I want to step out into some
fresh morning and look around and hear myself
crying out: "The house of money is falling!
The house of money is falling! The weeds are
rising! The weeds are rising!"

PRAYER

May I never not be frisky,
May I never not be risqué.

May my ashes, when you have them, friend,
and give them to the ocean,

leap in the froth of the waves,
still loving movement,

still ready, beyond all else,
to dance for the world.

MYSTERIES, YES

Truly, we live with mysteries too marvelous
    to be understood.

How grass can be nourishing in the
    mouths of the lambs.
How rivers and stones are forever
    in allegiance with gravity
        while we ourselves dream of rising.
How two hands touch and the bonds will
    never be broken.
How people come, from delight or the
    scars of damage,
to the comfort of a poem.

Let me keep my distance, always, from those
    who think they have the answers.

Let me keep company always with those who say
    "Look!" and laugh in astonishment,
    and bow their heads.

AT THE RIVER CLARION

I don't know who God is exactly.
But I'll tell you this.
I was sitting in the river named Clarion, on a
    water splashed stone
and all afternoon I listened to the voices
    of the river talking.
Whenever the water struck the stone it had
    something to say,
and the water itself, and even the mosses trailing
    under the water.
And slowly, very slowly, it became clear to me
    what they were saying.
Said the river: I am part of holiness.
And I too, said the stone. And I too, whispered
    the moss beneath the water.

I'd been to the river before, a few times.
Don't blame the river that nothing happened quickly.
You don't hear such voices in an hour or a day.
You don't hear them at all if selfhood has stuffed your ears.
And it's difficult to hear anything anyway, through
    all the traffic, and ambition.

2.

If God exists he isn't just butter and good luck.
He's also the tick that killed my wonderful dog Luke.
Said the river: imagine everything you can imagine, then
    keep on going.

Imagine how the lily (who may also be a part of God)
     would sing to you if it could sing, if
          you would pause to hear it.
And how are you so certain anyway that it doesn't sing?

If God exists he isn't just churches and mathematics.
He's the forest, He's the desert.
He's the ice caps, that are dying.
He's the ghetto and the Museum of Fine Arts.

He's van Gogh and Allen Ginsberg and Robert
     Motherwell.
He's the many desperate hands, cleaning and preparing
     their weapons.
He's every one of us, potentially.
The leaf of grass, the genius, the politician,
     the poet.
And if this is true, isn't it something very important?

Yes, it could be that I am a tiny piece of God, and
     each of you too, or at least
          of his intention and his hope.
Which is a delight beyond measure.
I don't know how you get to suspect such an idea.
     I only know that the river kept singing.
It wasn't a persuasion, it was all the river's own
     constant joy
which was better by far than a lecture, which was
     comfortable, exciting, unforgettable.

3.

Of course for each of us, there is the daily life.
Let us live it, gesture by gesture.
When we cut the ripe melon, should we not give it thanks?
And should we not thank the knife also?
We do not live in a simple world.

4.

There was someone I loved who grew old and ill.
One by one I watched the fires go out.
There was nothing I could do

except to remember
that we receive
then we give back.

5.

My dog Luke lies in a grave in the forest,
   she is given back.
But the river Clarion still flows
   from wherever it comes from
      to where it has been told to go.
I pray for the desperate earth.
I pray for the desperate world.
I do the little each person can do, it isn't much.
Sometimes the river murmurs, sometimes it raves.

6.

Along its shores were, may I say, very intense
    cardinal flowers.
And trees, and birds that have wings to uphold them,
    for heaven's sakes—
the lucky ones: they have such deep natures,
    they are so happily obedient.
While I sit here in a house filled with books,
    ideas, doubts, hesitations.

7.

And still, pressed deep into my mind, the river
    keeps coming, touching me, passing by on its
        long journey, its pale, infallible voice
            singing.

FROM

The Truro Bear and Other Adventures

2008

THE OTHER KINGDOMS

Consider the other kingdoms. The
trees, for example, with their mellow-sounding
titles: oak, aspen, willow.
Or the snow, for which the peoples of the north
have dozens of words to describe its
different arrivals. Or the creatures, with their
thick fur, their shy and wordless gaze. Their
infallible sense of what their lives
are meant to be. Thus the world
grows rich, grows wild, and you too,
grow rich, grow sweetly wild, as you too
were born to be.

THE GIFT

After the wind-bruised sea
   furrowed itself back
      into folds of blue, I found
      in the black wrack

a shell called the Neptune—
   tawny and white,
     spherical,
       with a tail

and a tower
   and a dark door,
     and all of it
      no larger

than my fist.
   It looked, you might say,
     very expensive.
      I thought of its travels

in the Atlantic's
   wind-pounded bowl
     and wondered
      that it was still intact.

Ah yes, there was
   that door
     that held only the eventual, inevitable
      emptiness.

. . .

There's that—there's always that.
   Still, what a house
      to leave behind!
         I held it

like the wisest of books
   and imagined
      its travels toward my hand.
      And now, your hand.

COYOTE IN THE DARK,
COYOTES REMEMBERED

The darkest thing

met me in the dark.

It was only a face

and a brace of teeth

that held no words,

though I felt a salty breath

sighing in my direction.

Once, in an autumn that is long gone,

I was down on my knees

in the cranberry bog

and heard, in that lonely place,

two voices coming down the hill,

and I was thrilled

to be granted this secret,

that the coyotes, walking together

can talk together,

for I thought, what else could it be?

And even though what emerged

were two young women, two-legged for sure

and not at all aware of me,

their nimble, young women tongues

telling and answering,

and though I knew

I had believed something probably not true,

yet it was wonderful

to have believed it.

And it has stayed with me

as a present once given is forever given.
Easy and happy they sounded,
those two maidens of the wilderness
from which we have—
who knows to what furious, pitiful extent—
banished ourselves.

FROM

Red Bird

2008

NIGHT HERONS

Some herons
were fishing
in the robes
of the night

at a low hour
of the water's body,
and the fish, I suppose,
were full

of fish happiness
in those transparent inches
even as, over and over,
the beaks jacked down

and the narrow
bodies were lifted
with every
quick sally,

and that was the end of them
as far as we know—
though, what do we know
except that death

is so everywhere and so entire—
pummeling and felling,
or sometimes,
like this, appearing

through such a thin door—
one stab, and you're through!
And what then?
Why, then it was almost morning,

and one by one
the birds
opened their wings
and flew.

MORNINGS AT BLACKWATER

For years, every morning, I drank
from Blackwater Pond.
It was flavored with oak leaves and also, no doubt,
the feet of ducks.

And always it assuaged me
from the dry bowl of the very far past.

What I want to say is
that the past is the past,
and the present is what your life is,
and you are capable
of choosing what that will be,
darling citizen.

So come to the pond,
or the river of your imagination,
or the harbor of your longing,

and put your lips to the world.
And live
your life.

THE ORCHARD

I have dreamed
of accomplishment.
I have fed

ambition.
I have traded
nights of sleep

for a length of work.
Lo, and I have discovered
how soft bloom

turns to green fruit
which turns to sweet fruit.
Lo, and I have discovered

all winds blow cold
at last,
and the leaves,

so pretty, so many,
vanish
in the great, black

packet of time,
in the great, black
packet of ambition,

and the ripeness
of the apple
is its downfall.

SOMETIMES

1.

Something came up
out of the dark.
It wasn't anything I had ever seen before.
It wasn't an animal
      or a flower,
unless it was both.

Something came up out of the water,
      a head the size of a cat
but muddy and without ears.
I don't know what God is.
I don't know what death is.

But I believe they have between them
      some fervent and necessary arrangement.

2.

Sometimes
melancholy leaves me breathless.

3.

Later I was in a field full of sunflowers.
I was feeling the heat of midsummer.
I was thinking of the sweet, electric
      drowse of creation,

when it began to break.

. . .

In the west, clouds gathered.
Thunderheads.
In an hour the sky was filled with them.

In an hour the sky was filled
    with the sweetness of rain and the blast of lightning.
Followed by the deep bells of thunder.

Water from the heavens! Electricity from the source!
Both of them mad to create something!

The lightning brighter than any flower.
The thunder without a drowsy bone in its body.

4.

Instructions for living a life:
Pay attention.
Be astonished.
Tell about it.

5.

Two or three times in my life I discovered love.
Each time it seemed to solve everything.
Each time it solved a great many things
    but not everything.
Yet left me as grateful as if it had indeed, and
thoroughly, solved everything.

6.

God, rest in my heart
and fortify me,
take away my hunger for answers,
let the hours play upon my body

like the hands of my beloved.
Let the cathead appear again—
the smallest of your mysteries,
some wild cousin of my own blood probably—
some cousin of my own wild blood probably,
in the black dinner-bowl of the pond.

7.

Death waits for me, I know it, around
       one corner or another.
This doesn't amuse me.
Neither does it frighten me.

After the rain, I went back into the field of sunflowers.
It was cool, and I was anything but drowsy.
I walked slowly, and listened

to the crazy roots, in the drenched earth, laughing and growing.

INVITATION

Oh do you have time
 to linger
  for just a little while
  out of your busy

and very important day
 for the goldfinches
  that have gathered
  in a field of thistles

for a musical battle,
 to see who can sing
  the highest note,
  or the lowest,

or the most expressive of mirth,
 or the most tender?
  Their strong, blunt beaks
  drink the air

as they strive
 melodiously
  not for your sake
  and not for mine

and not for the sake of winning
 but for sheer delight and gratitude—
  believe us, they say,
  it is a serious thing

just to be alive
   on this fresh morning
      in this broken world.
         I beg of you,

do not walk by
   without pausing
      to attend to this
         rather ridiculous performance.

It could mean something.
   It could mean everything.
      It could be what Rilke meant, when he wrote:
         You must change your life.

FROM THIS RIVER, WHEN I WAS A CHILD, I USED TO DRINK

But when I came back I found
that the body of the river was dying.

"Did it speak?"

Yes, it sang out the old songs, but faintly.

"What will you do?"

I will grieve of course, but that's nothing.

"What, precisely, will you grieve for?"

For the river. For myself, my lost
joyfulness. For the children who will not
know what a river can be—a friend, a
companion, a hint of heaven.

"Isn't this somewhat overplayed?"

I said: it can be a friend. A companion. A
hint of heaven.

WE SHOULD BE WELL PREPARED

The way the plovers cry goodbye.

The way the dead fox keeps on looking down the hill
    with open eye.

The way the leaves fall, and then there's the long wait.

The way someone says: we must never meet again.

The way mold spots the cake,

the way sourness overtakes the cream.

The way the river water rushes by, never to return.

The way the days go by, never to return.

The way somebody comes back, but only in a dream.

MEADOWLARK SINGS AND I
GREET HIM IN RETURN

Meadowlark, when you sing it's as if
you lay your yellow breast upon mine and say
hello, hello, and are we not
of one family, in our delight of life?
You sing, I listen.
Both are necessary
if the world is to continue going around
night-heavy then light-laden, though not
everyone knows this or at least
not yet,

or, perhaps, has forgotten it
in the torn fields,

in the terrible debris of progress.

OF THE EMPIRE

We will be known as a culture that feared death
and adored power, that tried to vanquish insecurity
for the few and cared little for the penury of the
many. We will be known as a culture that taught
and rewarded the amassing of things, that spoke
little if at all about the quality of life for
people (other people), for dogs, for rivers. All
the world, in our eyes, they will say, was a
commodity. And they will say that this structure
was held together politically, which it was, and
they will say also that our politics was no more
than an apparatus to accommodate the feelings of
the heart, and that the heart, in those days,
was small, and hard, and full of meanness.

RED

All the while
I was teaching
in the state of Virginia
I wanted to see
gray fox.
Finally I found him.
He was in the highway.
He was singing
his death song.
I picked him up
and carried him
into a field
while the cars kept coming.
He showed me
how he could ripple
how he could bleed.
Goodbye I said
to the light of his eye
as the cars went by.
Two mornings later
I found the other.
She was in the highway.
She was singing
her death song.
I picked her up
and carried her
into the field
where she rippled
half of her gray

half of her red
while the cars kept coming.
While the cars kept coming.
Gray fox and gray fox.
Red, red, red.

NIGHT AND THE RIVER

I have seen the great feet
leaping
into the river

and I have seen moonlight
milky
along the long muzzle

and I have seen the body
of something
scaled and wonderful

slumped in the sudden fire of its mouth,
and I could not tell
which fit me

more comfortably, the power,
or the powerlessness;
neither would have me

entirely; I was divided,
consumed,
by sympathy,

pity, admiration.
After a while
it was done,

the fish had vanished, the bear
lumped away
to the green shore

. . .

and into the trees. And then there was only
this story.
It followed me home

and entered my house—
a difficult guest
with a single tune

which it hums all day and through the night—
slowly or briskly,
it doesn't matter,

it sounds like a river leaping and falling;
it sounds like a body
falling apart.

SELF-PORTRAIT

I wish I was twenty and in love with life
   and still full of beans.

Onward, old legs!
There are the long, pale dunes; on the other side
the roses are blooming and finding their labor
no adversity to the spirit.

Upward, old legs! There are the roses, and there is the sea
shining like a song, like a body
I want to touch

though I'm not twenty
and won't be again but ah! seventy. And still
in love with life. And still
full of beans.

WITH THE BLACKEST OF INKS

At night
   the panther,
      who is lean
         and quick,

is only
   a pair of eyes
      and, with a yawn,
         momentarily,

a long, pink tongue.
   Mostly
      he listens
         as he walks

on the puffs
   of his feet
      as if
         on a carpet

from Persia,
   or leaps
      into the branches
         of a tree,

or swims
   across the river,
      or simply
         stands in the grass

. . .

and waits.
    Because, Sir,
        you have given him,
            for your own reasons,

everything that he needs:
    leaves, food, shelter;
        a conscience
            that never blinks.

FROM

Thirst

2006

WHEN I AM AMONG THE TREES

When I am among the trees,
especially the willows and the honey locust,
equally the beech, the oaks and the pines,
they give off such hints of gladness.
I would almost say that they save me, and daily.

I am so distant from the hope of myself,
in which I have goodness, and discernment,
and never hurry through the world
    but walk slowly, and bow often.

Around me the trees stir in their leaves
and call out, "Stay awhile."
The light flows from their branches.

And they call again, "It's simple," they say,
"and you too have come
into the world to do this, to go easy, to be filled
with light, and to shine."

WHEN THE ROSES SPEAK, I PAY ATTENTION

"As long as we are able to
be extravagant we will be
hugely and damply
extravagant. Then we will drop
foil by foil to the ground. This
is our unalterable task, and we do it
joyfully."

And they went on. "Listen,
the heart-shackles are not, as you think,
death, illness, pain,
unrequited hope, not loneliness, but

lassitude, rue, vainglory, fear, anxiety,
selfishness."

Their fragrance all the while rising
from their blind bodies, making me
spin with joy.

SIX RECOGNITIONS OF THE LORD

1.

I know a lot of fancy words.
I tear them from my heart and my tongue.
Then I pray.

2.

Lord God, mercy is in your hands, pour
me a little. And tenderness too. My
need is great. Beauty walks so freely
and with such gentleness. Impatience puts
a halter on my face and I run away over
the green fields wanting your voice, your
tenderness, but having to do with only
the sweet grasses of the fields against
my body. When I first found you I was
filled with light, now the darkness grows
and it is filled with crooked things, bitter
and weak, each one bearing my name.

3.

I lounge on the grass, that's all. So
simple. Then I lie back until I am
inside the cloud that is just above me
but very high, and shaped like a fish.
Or, perhaps not. Then I enter the place
of not-thinking, not-remembering, not-
wanting. When the blue jay cries out his

riddle, in his carping voice, I return.
But I go back, the threshold is always
near. Over and back, over and back. Then
I rise. Maybe I rub my face as though I
have been asleep. But I have not been
asleep. I have been, as I say, inside
the cloud, or, perhaps, the lily floating
on the water. Then I go back to town,
to my own house, my own life, which has
now become brighter and simpler, some-
where I have never been before.

4.

Of course I have always known you
are present in the clouds, and the
black oak I especially adore, and the
wings of birds. But you are present
too in the body, listening to the body,
teaching it to live, instead of all
that touching, with disembodied joy.
We do not do this easily. We have
lived so long in the heaven of touch,
and we maintain our mutability, our
physicality, even as we begin to
apprehend the other world. Slowly we
make our appreciative response.
Slowly appreciation swells to
astonishment. And we enter the dialogue

of our lives that is beyond all under-
standing or conclusion. It is mystery.
It is love of God. It is obedience.

5.

Oh, feed me this day, Holy Spirit, with
the fragrance of the fields and the
freshness of the oceans which you have
made, and help me to hear and to hold
in all dearness those exacting and wonderful
words of our Lord Christ Jesus, saying:
Follow me.

6.

Every summer the lilies rise
    and open their white hands until they almost
cover the black waters of the pond. And I give
    thanks but it does not seem like adequate thanks,
it doesn't seem
    festive enough or constant enough, nor does the
name of the Lord or the words of thanksgiving come
    into it often enough. Everywhere I go I am
treated like royalty, which I am not. I thirst and
    am given water. My eyes thirst and I am given
the white lilies on the black water. My heart
    sings but the apparatus of singing doesn't convey
half what it feels and means. In spring there's hope,
    in fall the exquisite, necessary diminishing, in

winter I am as sleepy as any beast in its
    leafy cave, but in summer there is
everywhere the luminous sprawl of gifts,
    the hospitality of the Lord and my
inadequate answers as I row my beautiful, temporary body
    through this water-lily world.

GETHSEMANE

The grass never sleeps.
Or the roses.
Nor does the lily have a secret eye that shuts until morning.

Jesus said, wait with me. But the disciples slept.

The cricket has such splendid fringe on its feet,
and it sings, have you noticed, with its whole body,
and heaven knows if it ever sleeps.

Jesus said, wait with me. And maybe the stars did, maybe
the wind wound itself into a silver tree, and didn't move,
    maybe
the lake far away, where once he walked as on a
    blue pavement,
lay still and waited, wild awake.

Oh the dear bodies, slumped and eye-shut, that could not
keep that vigil, how they must have wept,
so utterly human, knowing this too
must be a part of the story.

THE POET THINKS ABOUT THE DONKEY

On the outskirts of Jerusalem
the donkey waited.
Not especially brave, or filled with understanding,
he stood and waited.

How horses, turned out into the meadow,
  leap with delight!
How doves, released from their cages,
  clatter away, splashed with sunlight!

But the donkey, tied to a tree as usual, waited.
Then he let himself be led away.
Then he let the stranger mount.

Never had he seen such crowds!
And I wonder if he at all imagined what was to happen.
Still, he was what he had always been: small, dark, obedient.

I hope, finally, he felt brave.
I hope, finally, he loved the man who rode so lightly upon him,
as he lifted one dusty hoof and stepped, as he had to, forward.

PRAYING

It doesn't have to be
the blue iris, it could be
weeds in a vacant lot, or a few
small stones; just
pay attention, then patch

a few words together and don't try
to make them elaborate, this isn't
a contest but the doorway

into thanks, and a silence in which
another voice may speak.

DOESN'T EVERY POET WRITE
A POEM ABOUT UNREQUITED LOVE?

The flowers
   I wanted to bring to you,
      wild and wet
         from the pale dunes

and still smelling
   of the summer night,
      and still holding a moment or two
         of the night cricket's

humble prayer,
   would have been
      so handsome
         in your hands—

so happy—I dare to say it—
   in your hands—
      yet your smile
         would have been nowhere

and maybe you would have tossed them
   onto the ground,
      or maybe, for tenderness,
         you would have taken them

into your house
   and given them water
      and put them in a dark corner
         out of reach.

In matters of love
  of this kind
    there are things we long to do
      but must not do.

I would not want to see
  your smile diminished.
    And the flowers, anyway,
      are happy just where they are,

on the pale dunes,
  above the cricket's humble nest,
    under the blue sky
      that loves us all.

ON THY WONDROUS WORKS
I WILL MEDITATE

(Psalm 145)

1.

All day up and down the shore the
    fine points of the waves keep on
tapping whatever is there: scatter of broken
    clams, empty jingles, old
oyster shells thick and castellated that held
    once the pale jewel of their bodies, such sweet

tongue and juice. And who do you
    think you are sauntering along
five feet up in the air, the ocean a blue fire
    around your ankles, the sun
on your face on your shoulders its golden mouth whispering
    (so it seems) *you! you! you!*

2.

Now the afternoon wind
    all frill and no apparent purpose
takes her cloud-shaped
    hand and touches every one of the
waves so that rapidly
    they stir the wings of the eiders they blur

the boats on their moorings; not even the rocks
    black and blunt interrupt the waves on their

way to the shore and one last swimmer (is it you?) rides
    their salty infoldings and outfoldings until,
peaked, their blue sides heaving, they pause; and God
    whistles them back; and you glide safely to shore.

3.

One morning
    a hundred pink and cylindrical
squid lay beached their lacy faces,
    their gnarls of dimples and ropy tentacles
limp and powerless; as I watched
    the big gulls went down upon

this sweetest trash rolling
    like the arms of babies through the
swash—in a feathered dash,
    a calligraphy of delight the beaks fell
grabbing and snapping; then was left only the
    empty beach, the birds floating back over the waves.

4.

How many mysteries have you seen in your
    lifetime? How many nets pulled
full over the boat's side, each silver body
    ready or not falling into
submission? How many roses in early summer
    uncurling above the pale sands then

. . .

falling back in unfathomable
    willingness? And what can you say? Glory
to the rose and the leaf, to the seed, to the
    silver fish. Glory to time and the wild fields,
and to joy. And to grief's shock and torpor, its near swoon.

5.

So it is not hard to understand
    where God's body is, it is
everywhere and everything; shore and the vast
    fields of water, the accidental and the intended
over here, over there. And I bow down
    participate and attentive

it is so dense and apparent. And all the same I am still
    unsatisfied. Standing
here, now, I am thinking
    not of His thick wrists and His blue
shoulders but, still, of Him. Where, do you suppose, is His
    pale and wonderful mind?

6.

I would be good—oh, I would be upright and good.
    To what purpose? To be shining not
sinful, not wringing out of the hours
    petulance, heaviness, ashes. *To what purpose?*

Hope of heaven? Not that. But to enter
   the other kingdom: grace, and imagination,

and the multiple sympathies: to be as a leaf, a rose,
   a dolphin, a wave rising
slowly then briskly out of the darkness to touch
   the limpid air, to be God's mind's
servant, loving with the body's sweet mouth—its kisses, its
words—
   everything.

7.

I know a man of such
   mildness and kindness it is trying to
change my life. He does not
   preach, teach, but simply is. It is
astonishing, for he is Christ's ambassador
   truly, by rule and act. But, more,

he is kind with the sort of kindness that shines
   out, but is resolute, not fooled. He has
eaten the dark hours and could also, I think,
   soldier for God, riding out
under the storm clouds, against the world's pride and unkindness
   with both unassailable sweetness, and consoling word.

8.

Every morning I want to kneel down on the golden
    cloth of the sand and say
some kind of musical thanks for
    the world that is happening again—another day—
from the shawl of wind coming out of the
    west to the firm green

flesh of the melon lately sliced open and
    eaten, its chill and ample body
flavored with mercy. I want
    to be worthy of—what? Glory? Yes, unimaginable glory.
O Lord of melons, of mercy, though I am
    not ready, nor worthy, I am climbing toward you.

THE CHAT

I wish
  I were
    the yellow chat
      down in the thickets

who sings all night,
  throwing
    into the air
      praises

and panhandles,
  plaints,
    in curly phrases,
      half-rhymes,

free verse too,
  with head-dipping
    and wing-wringing,
      with soft breast

rising into the air—
  meek and sleek,
    broadcasting,
      with no time out

for pillow-rest,
  everything—
    pathos,
      thanks—

. . .

oh, Lord,
    what a lesson
        you send me
            as I stand

listening
    to your rattling, swamp-loving chat
        singing
            of his simple, leafy life—

how I would like to sing to you
    all night
        in the dark
            just like that.

THIRST

Another morning and I wake with thirst
for the goodness I do not have. I walk
out to the pond and all the way God has
given us such beautiful lessons. Oh Lord,
I was never a quick scholar but sulked
and hunched over my books past the
hour and the bell; grant me, in your
mercy, a little more time. Love for the
earth and love for you are having such a
long conversation in my heart. Who
knows what will finally happen or
where I will be sent, yet already I have
given a great many things away, expect-
ing to be told to pack nothing, except the
prayers which, with this thirst, I am
slowly learning.

FROM

New and
Selected Poems:
Volume Two

2005

HUM

What is this dark hum among the roses?
    The bees have gone simple, sipping,
that's all. What did you expect? Sophistication?
    They're small creatures and they are
filling their bodies with sweetness, how could they not
    moan in happiness? The little
worker bee lives, I have read, about three weeks.
    Is that long? Long enough, I suppose, to understand
that life is a blessing. I have found them—haven't you?—
    stopped in the very cups of the flowers, their wings
a little tattered—so much flying about, to the hive,
    then out into the world, then back, and perhaps dancing,
should the task be to be a scout—sweet, dancing bee.
    I think there isn't anything in this world I don't
admire. If there is, I don't know what it is. I
    haven't met it yet. Nor expect to. The bee is small,
and since I wear glasses, so I can see the traffic and
    read books, I have to
take them off and bend close to study and
    understand what is happening. It's not hard, it's in fact
as instructive as anything I have ever studied. Plus, too,
    it's love almost too fierce to endure, the bee
nuzzling like that into the blouse
    of the rose. And the fragrance, and the honey, and of course
the sun, the purely pure sun, shining, all the while, over
    all of us.

LEAD

Here is a story
to break your heart.
Are you willing?
This winter
the loons came to our harbor
and died, one by one,
of nothing we could see.
A friend told me
of one on the shore
that lifted its head and opened
the elegant beak and cried out
in the long, sweet savoring of its life
which, if you have heard it,
you know is a sacred thing,
and for which, if you have not heard it,
you had better hurry to where
they still sing.
And, believe me, tell no one
just where that is.
The next morning
this loon, speckled
and iridescent and with a plan
to fly home
to some hidden lake,
was dead on the shore.
I tell you this
to break your heart,

by which I mean only

that it break open and never close again

to the rest of the world.

OXYGEN

Everything needs it: bone, muscles, and even,
while it calls the earth its home, the soul.
So the merciful, noisy machine

stands in our house working away in its
lung-like voice. I hear it as I kneel
before the fire, stirring with a

stick of iron, letting the logs
lie more loosely. You, in the upstairs room,
are in your usual position, leaning on your

right shoulder which aches
all day. You are breathing
patiently; it is a

beautiful sound. It is
your life, which is so close
to my own that I would not know

where to drop the knife of
separation. And what does this have to do
with love, except

everything? Now the fire rises
and offers a dozen, singing, deep-red
roses of flame. Then it settles

to quietude, or maybe gratitude, as it feeds
as we all do, as we must, upon the invisible gift:
our purest, sweet necessity: the air.

WHITE HERON RISES OVER BLACKWATER

I wonder
   what it is
      that I will accomplish
         today

if anything
   can be called
      that marvelous word.
         It won't be

my kind of work,
   which is only putting
      words on a page,
         the pencil

haltingly calling up
   the light of the world,
      yet nothing appearing on paper
         half as bright

as the mockingbird's
   verbal hilarity
      in the still unleafed shrub
         in the churchyard—

or the white heron
   rising
      over the swamp
         and the darkness,

. . .

his yellow eyes
    and broad wings wearing
        the light of the world
            in the light of the world—

ah yes, I see him.
    He is exactly
        the poem
            I wanted to write.

Who can tell how lovely in June is the
    honey locust tree, or why
a tree should be so sweet and live
    in this world? Each white blossom
on a dangle of white flowers holds one green seed—
    a new life. Also each blossom on a dangle of flowers
      holds a flask
of fragrance called *Heaven*, which is never sealed.
    The bees circle the tree and dive into it. They are crazy
with gratitude. They are working like farmers. They are as
    happy as saints. After a while the flowers begin to
wilt and drop down into the grass. Welcome
    shines in the grass.

          Every year I gather
handfuls of blossoms and eat of their mealiness; the honey
    melts in my mouth, the seeds make me strong,
both when they are crisp and ripe, and even at the end
    when their petals have turned dull yellow.

               So it is

if the heart has devoted itself to love, there is
    not a single inch of emptiness. Gladness gleams
all the way to the grave.

SONG FOR AUTUMN

In the deep fall
    don't you imagine the leaves think how
comfortable it will be to touch
    the earth instead of the
nothingness of air and the endless
    freshets of wind? And don't you think
the trees themselves, especially those with mossy,
    warm caves, begin to think

of the birds that will come—six, a dozen—to sleep
    inside their bodies? And don't you hear
the goldenrod whispering goodbye,
    the everlasting being crowned with the first
tuffets of snow? The pond
    vanishes, and the white field over which
the fox runs so quickly brings out
    its blue shadows. And the wind pumps its
bellows. And at evening especially,
    the piled firewood shifts a little,
longing to be on its way.

FIREFLIES

At Blackwater
fireflies
are not even a dime a dozen—
they are free,

and each floats and turns
among the branches of the oaks
and the swamp azaleas
looking for another

as, who doesn't?
Oh, blessings
on the intimacy
inside fruition,

be it foxes
or the fireflies
or the dampness inside the petals
of a thousand flowers.

Though Eden is lost
its loveliness
remains in the heart
and the imagination;

he would take her
in a boat
over the dark water;
she would take him

. . .

to an island she knows
where the blue flag grows wild
and the grass is deep,
where the birds

perch together,
feather to feather,
on the bough.
And the fireflies,

blinking their little lights,
hurry toward one another.
And the world continues,
God willing.

THE POET WITH HIS FACE IN HIS HANDS

You want to cry aloud for your
mistakes. But to tell the truth the world
doesn't need any more of that sound.

So if you're going to do it and can't
stop yourself, if your pretty mouth can't
hold it in, at least go by yourself across

the forty fields and the forty dark inclines
of rocks and water to the place where
the falls are flinging out their white sheets

like crazy, and there is a cave behind all that
jubilation and water-fun and you can
stand there, under it, and roar all you

want and nothing will be disturbed; you can
drip with despair all afternoon and still,
on a green branch, its wings just lightly touched

by the passing foil of the water, the thrush,
puffing out its spotted breast, will sing
of the perfect, stone-hard beauty of everything.

WILD, WILD

This is what love is:
the dry rose bush the gardener, in his pruning, missed
suddenly bursts into bloom.
A madness of delight; an obsession.
A holy gift, certainly.
But often, alas, improbable.

Why couldn't Romeo have settled for someone else?
Why couldn't Tristan and Isolde have refused
the shining cup
which would have left peaceful the whole kingdom?

Wild sings the bird of the heart in the forests
    of our lives.

Over and over Faust, standing in the garden, doesn't know
anything that's going to happen, he only sees
    the face of Marguerite, which is irresistible.

And wild, wild sings the bird.

NORTH COUNTRY

In the north country now it is spring and there
    is a certain celebration. The thrush
has come home. He is shy and likes the
    evening best, also the hour just before
morning; in that blue and gritty light he
    climbs to his branch, or smoothly
sails there. It is okay to know only
    one song if it is this one. Hear it
rise and fall; the very elements of your soul
    shiver nicely. What would spring be
without it? Mostly frogs. But don't worry, he

arrives, year after year, humble and obedient
    and gorgeous. You listen and you know
you could live a better life than you do, be
    softer, kinder. And maybe this year you will
be able to do it. Hear how his voice
    rises and falls. There is no way to be
sufficiently grateful for the gifts we are
    given, no way to speak the Lord's name
often enough, though we do try, and

especially now, as that dappled breast
    breathes in the pines and heaven's
windows in the north country, now spring has come,
    are opened wide.

TERNS

Don't think just now of the trudging forward of thought,
but of the wing-drive of unquestioning affirmation.

It's summer, you never saw such a blue sky,
and here they are, those white birds with quick wings,

sweeping over the waves,
chattering and plunging,

their thin beaks snapping, their hard eyes
happy as little nails.

The years to come—this is a promise—
will grant you ample time

to try the difficult steps in the empire of thought
where you seek for the shining proofs you think you must have.

But nothing you ever understand will be sweeter, or more binding,
than this deepest affinity between your eyes and the world.

The flock thickens
over the roiling, salt brightness. Listen,

maybe such devotion, in which one holds the world
in the clasp of attention, isn't the perfect prayer,

but it must be close, for the sorrow, whose name is doubt,
is thus subdued, and not through the weaponry of reason,

. . .

but of pure submission. Tell me, what else
could beauty be for? And now the tide

is at its very crown,
the white birds sprinkle down,

gathering up the loose silver, rising
as if weightless. It isn't instruction, or a parable.

It isn't for any vanity or ambition
except for the one allowed, to stay alive.

It's only a nimble frolic
over the waves. And you find, for hours,

you cannot even remember the questions
that weigh so in your mind.

Blue Iris

JUST LYING ON THE GRASS
AT BLACKWATER

I think sometimes of the possible glamour of death—
that it might be wonderful to be
lost and happy inside the green grass—
or to be the green grass!—
or, maybe the pink rose, or the blue iris,
or the affable daisy, or the twirled vine
looping its way skyward—that it might be perfectly peaceful
to be the shining lake, or the hurrying, athletic river,
or the dark shoulders of the trees
where the thrush each evening weeps himself into an ecstasy.

I lie down in the fields of goldenrod, and everlasting.
Who could find me?
My thoughts simplify. I have not done a thousand things
or a hundred things but, perhaps, a few.
As for wondering about answers that are not available except
in books, though all my childhood I was sent there
to find them, I have learned
to leave all that behind

as in summer I take off my shoes and my socks,
my jacket, my hat, and go on
happier, through the fields. The little sparrow
with the pink beak
calls out, over and over, so simply—not to me

but to the whole world. All afternoon
I grow wiser, listening to him,

soft, small, nameless fellow at the top of some weed,
enjoying his life. If you can sing, do it. If not,

even silence can feel, to the world, like happiness,
like praise,
from the pool of shade you have found beneath the everlasting.

SEA LEAVES

I walk beside the ocean, then turn and continue walking just beside the first berm, a few yards from the water which is at half tide. Eventually I find what I'm looking for, a plant green and with the flavor of raw salt, and leaves shaped like arrow-heads. But before that, down the long shore, I have seen many things: shells, waves, once a pair of whimbrels, gulls and terns over the water, rabbits long-legging it through the thickets above the berm. I kneel and pick among the green leaves, not taking all of any plant but a few leaves from each, until my knapsack is filled. Keep your spinach; I'll have this. Then I stroll home. I'll cook the leaves briefly; M. and I will eat some and put the rest into the freezer, for winter. The only thing I don't know is, should the activity of this day be called labor, or pleasure?

MORNING AT BLACKWATER

It's almost dawn
and the usual half-miracles begin
within my own personal body as the light
enters the gates of the east and climbs
into the fields of the sky, and the birds lift
their very unimportant heads from the branches
and begin to sing; and the insects too,
and the rustling leaves, and even
that most common of earthly things, the grass,
can't let it begin—another morning—without
making some comment of gladness, respiring softly
with the honey of their green bodies; and the white
blossoms of the swamp honeysuckle, hovering just where
the path and the pond almost meet,
shake from the folds of their bodies
such happiness it enters the air as fragrance,
the day's first pale and elegant affirmation.
And the old gods liked so well, they say,
the sweet odor of prayer.

HOW WOULD YOU LIVE THEN?

What if a hundred rose-breasted grosbeaks
    flew in circles around your head? What if
the mockingbird came into the house with you and
    became your advisor? What if
the bees filled your walls with honey and all
    you needed to do was ask them and they would fill
the bowl? What if the brook slid downhill just
    past your bedroom window so you could listen
to its slow prayers as you fell asleep? What if
    the stars began to shout their names, or to run
this way and that way above the clouds? What if
    you painted a picture of a tree, and the leaves
began to rustle, and a bird cheerfully sang
    from its painted branches? What if you suddenly saw
that the silver of water was brighter than the silver
    of money? What if you finally saw
that the sunflowers, turning toward the sun all day
    and every day—who knows how, but they do it—were
more precious, more meaningful than gold?

HOW THE GRASS AND THE FLOWERS CAME
TO EXIST, A GOD-TALE

I suppose
the Lord said:
Let there be fur upon the earth,
and let there be hair upon the earth,

and so the seeds stuttered forward into ripeness
and the roots twirled in the dark
to accomplish His desire,

and so there is clover,
and the reeds of the marshes,
and the eelgrass of the sea shallows
upon which the dainty sea brant live,

and there is the green and sturdy grass,
and the goldenrod
and the spurge and the yarrow
and the ivies and the bramble
and the blue iris

covering the earth,
thanking the Lord with their blossoms.

FROM

Why I Wake Early

2004

WHY I WAKE EARLY

Hello, sun in my face.
Hello, you who make the morning
and spread it over the fields
and into the faces of the tulips
and the nodding morning glories,
and into the windows of, even, the
miserable and the crotchety—

best preacher that ever was,
dear star, that just happens
to be where you are in the universe
to keep us from ever-darkness,
to ease us with warm touching,
to hold us in the great hands of light—
good morning, good morning, good morning.

Watch, now, how I start the day
in happiness, in kindness.

SPRING AT BLACKWATER:
I GO THROUGH THE LESSONS
ALREADY LEARNED

He gave the fish
her coat of foil,
and her soft eggs.
He made the kingfisher's
quick eye
and her peerless, terrible beak.
He made the circles
of the days and the seasons
to close tightly,
and forever—

then open again.

MINDFUL

Every day
    I see or I hear
        something
            that more or less

kills me
    with delight,
        that leaves me
            like a needle

in the haystack
    of light.
        It is what I was born for—
            to look, to listen,

to lose myself
    inside this soft world—
        to instruct myself
            over and over

in joy,
    and acclamation.
        Nor am I talking
            about the exceptional,

the fearful, the dreadful,
    the very extravagant—
        but of the ordinary,
            the common, the very drab,

the daily presentations.
    Oh, good scholar,
        I say to myself,
            how can you help

but grow wise
    with such teachings
        as these—
            the untrimmable light

of the world,
    the ocean's shine,
        the prayers that are made
            out of grass?

LINGERING IN HAPPINESS

After rain after many days without rain,
it stays cool, private and cleansed, under the trees,
and the dampness there, married now to gravity,
falls branch to branch, leaf to leaf, down to the ground

where it will disappear—but not, of course, vanish
except to our eyes. The roots of the oaks will have their share,
and the white threads of the grasses, and the cushion of moss;
a few drops, round as pearls, will enter the mole's tunnel;

and soon so many small stones, buried for a thousand years,
will feel themselves being touched.

DAISIES

It is possible, I suppose, that sometime
    we will learn everything
there is to learn: what the world is, for example,
    and what it means. I think this as I am crossing
from one field to another, in summer, and the
    mockingbird is mocking me, as one who either
knows enough already or knows enough to be
    perfectly content not knowing. Song being born
of quest he knows this: he must turn silent
    were he suddenly assaulted with answers. Instead

oh hear his wild, caustic, tender warbling ceaselessly
    unanswered. At my feet the white-petaled daisies display
the small suns of their center-piece—their, if you don't
    mind my saying so—their hearts. Of course
I could be wrong, perhaps their hearts are pale and
    narrow and hidden in the roots. What do I know.
But this: it is heaven itself to take what is given,
    to see what is plain; what the sun
lights up willingly; for example—I think this
    as I reach down, not to pick but merely to touch
the suitability of the field for the daisies, and the
    daisies for the field.

GOLDENROD, LATE FALL

This morning the goldenrod are all wearing
    their golden shirts
fresh from heaven's soft wash in the chill night.
    So it must be a celebration.
And here comes the wind, so many swinging wings!
    Has he been invited, or is he the intruder?
Invited, whisper the golden pebbles of the weeds,
    as they begin to fall

over the ground. Well, you would think the little murmurs
    of the broken blossoms would have said
otherwise, but no. So I sit down among them to
    think about it while all around me the crumbling
goes on. The weeds let down their seedy faces
    cheerfully, which is the part I like best, and certainly

it is as good as a book for learning from. You would think
    they were just going for a small sleep. You would think
they couldn't wait, it was going to be
    that snug and even, as all their lives were, full of
excitation. You would think

it was a voyage just beginning, and no darkness anywhere,
    but tinged with all necessary instruction, and light,

and all were shriven, as all the round world is,
    and so it wasn't anything but easy to fall, to whisper
Good Night.

THE OLD POETS OF CHINA

Wherever I am, the world comes after me.
It offers me its busyness. It does not believe
that I do not want it. Now I understand
why the old poets of China went so far and high
into the mountains, then crept into the pale mist.

LOGOS

Why wonder about the loaves and the fishes?
If you say the right words, the wine expands.
If you say them with love
and the felt ferocity of that love
and the felt necessity of that love,
the fish explode into many.
Imagine him, speaking,
and don't worry about what is reality,
or what is plain, or what is mysterious.
If you were there, it was all those things.
If you can imagine it, it is all those things.
Eat, drink, be happy.
Accept the miracle.
Accept, too, each spoken word
spoken with love.

SNOW GEESE

Oh, to love what is lovely, and will not last!
    What a task
        to ask

of anything, or anyone,

yet it is ours,
    and not by the century or the year, but by the hours.

One fall day I heard
    above me, and above the sting of the wind, a sound
I did not know, and my look shot upward; it was

a flock of snow geese, winging it
    faster than the ones we usually see,
and, being the color of snow, catching the sun

so they were, in part at least, golden. I

held my breath
as we do
sometimes
to stop time
when something wonderful
has touched us

as with a match
which is lit, and bright,
but does not hurt
in the common way,

. . .

but delightfully,
as if delight
were the most serious thing
you ever felt.

The geese
flew on.
I have never
seen them again.

Maybe I will, someday, somewhere.
Maybe I won't.
It doesn't matter.
What matters
is that, when I saw them,
I saw them
as through the veil, secretly, joyfully, clearly.

AT BLACK RIVER

All day
    its dark, slick bronze soaks
        in a mossy place,
            its teeth,

a multitude
    set
        for the comedy
            that never comes—

its tail
    knobbed and shiny,
        and with a heavy-weight's punch
            packed around the bone.

In beautiful Florida
    he is king
        of his own part
            of the black river,

and from his nap
    he will wake
        into the warm darkness
            to boom, and thrust forward,

paralyzing
    the swift, thin-waisted fish,
        or the bird
            in its frilled, white gown,

. . .

that has dipped down
   from the heaven of leaves
      one last time,
         to drink.

Don't think
   I'm not afraid.
      There is such an unleashing
         of horror.

Then I remember:
   death comes before
      the rolling away
         of the stone.

BEANS

They're not like peaches or squash. Plumpness isn't for them. They like being lean, as if for the narrow path. The beans themselves sit quietly inside their green pods. Instinctively one picks with care, never tearing down the fine vine, never not noticing their crisp bodies, or feeling their willingness for the pot, for the fire.

I have thought sometimes that something—I can't name it— watches as I walk the rows, accepting the gift of their lives to assist mine.

I know what you think: this is foolishness. They're only vegetables. Even the blossoms with which they begin are small and pale, hardly significant. Our hands, or minds, our feet hold more intelligence. With this I have no quarrel.

But, what about virtue?

THE ARROWHEAD

The arrowhead,
which I found beside the river,
was glittering and pointed.
I picked it up, and said,
"Now, it's mine."
I thought of showing it to friends.
I thought of putting it—such an imposing trinket—
in a little box, on my desk.
Halfway home, past the cut fields,
the old ghost
stood under the hickories.
"I would rather drink the wind," he said,
"I would rather eat mud and die
than steal as you still steal,
than lie as you still lie."

WHERE DOES THE TEMPLE BEGIN,
WHERE DOES IT END?

There are things you can't reach. But
you can reach out to them, and all day long.

The wind, the bird flying away. The idea of God.

And it can keep you as busy as anything else, and happier.

The snake slides away; the fish jumps, like a little lily,
out of the water and back in; the goldfinches sing
    from the unreachable top of the tree.

I look; morning to night I am never done with looking.

Looking I mean not just standing around, but standing around
    as though with your arms open.

And thinking: maybe something will come, some
    shining coil of wind,
        or a few leaves from any old tree—
            they are all in this too.

And now I will tell you the truth.
Everything in the world
comes.

At least, closer.

And, cordially.

. . .

Like the nibbling, tinsel-eyed fish; the unlooping snake.
Like goldfinches, little dolls of gold
fluttering around the corner of the sky

of God, the blue air.

FROM

Long Life

2004

JUST AS THE CALENDAR BEGAN
TO SAY SUMMER

I went out of the schoolhouse fast
and through the gardens and to the woods,
and spent all summer forgetting what I'd been taught—

two times two, and diligence, and so forth,
how to be modest and useful, and how to succeed and so forth,
machines and oil and plastic and money and so forth.

By fall I had healed somewhat, but was summoned back
to the chalky rooms and the desks, to sit and remember

the way the river kept rolling its pebbles,
the way the wild wrens sang though they hadn't a penny in the
    bank,
the way the flowers were dressed in nothing but light.

CAN YOU IMAGINE?

For example, what the trees do
not only in lightning storms
or the watery dark of a summer night
or under the white nets of winter
but now, and now, and now—whenever
we're not looking. Surely you can't imagine
they just stand there looking the way they look
when we're looking; surely you can't imagine
they don't dance, from the root up, wishing
to travel a little, not cramped so much as wanting
a better view, or more sun, or just as avidly
more shade—surely you can't imagine they just
stand there loving every
minute of it; the birds or the emptiness, the dark rings
of the years slowly and without a sound
thickening, and nothing different unless the wind,
and then only in its own mood, comes
to visit, surely you can't imagine
patience, and happiness, like that.

SOFTEST OF MORNINGS

Softest of mornings, hello.
And what will you do today, I wonder,
   to my heart?
And how much honey can the heart stand, I wonder,
   before it must break?

This is trivial, or nothing: a snail
   climbing a trellis of leaves
      and the blue trumpets of its flowers.

No doubt clocks are ticking loudly
   all over the world.
I don't hear them. The snail's pale horns
   extend and wave this way and that
as her finger-body shuffles forward, leaving behind
   the silvery path of her slime.

Oh, softest of mornings, how shall I break this?
How shall I move away from the snail, and the flowers?
How shall I go on, with my introspective and ambitious life?

CARRYING THE SNAKE TO THE GARDEN

In the cellar
was the smallest snake
I have ever seen.
It coiled itself
in a corner
and watched me
with eyes
like two little stars
set into coal,
and a tail
that quivered.
One step
of my foot
and it fled
like a running shoelace,
but a scoop of the wrist
and I had it
in my hand.
I was sorry
for the fear,
so I hurried
upstairs and out the kitchen door
to the warm grass
and the sunlight
and the garden.
It turned and turned
in my hand
but when I put it down
it didn't move.

I thought
it was going to flow
up my leg
and into my pocket.
I thought, for a moment,
as it lifted its face,
it was going to sing.

And then it was gone.

FROM

Owls and Other Fantasies

2003

THE DIPPER

Once I saw
in a quick-falling, white-veined stream,
among the leafed islands of the wet rocks,
a small bird, and knew it

from the pages of a book; it was
the dipper, and dipping he was,
as well as, sometimes, on a rock-peak, starting up
the clear, strong pipe of his voice; at this,

there being no words to transcribe, I had to
bend forward, as it were,
into his frame of mind, catching
everything I could in the tone,

cadence, sweetness, and briskness
of his affirmative report.
Though not by words, it was
a more than satisfactory way to the

bridge of understanding. This happened
in Colorado
more than half a century ago—
more, certainly, than half my lifetime ago—

and, just as certainly, he has been sleeping for decades
in the leaves beside the stream,
his crumble of white bones, his curl of flesh
comfortable even so.

. . .

And still I hear him—
and whenever I open the ponderous book of riddles
he sits with his black feet hooked to the page,
his eyes cheerful, still burning with water-love—

and thus the world is full of leaves and feathers,
and comfort, and instruction. I do not even remember
your name, great river,
but since that hour I have lived

simply,
in the joy of the body as full and clear
as falling water; the pleasures of the mind
like a dark bird dipping in and out, tasting and singing.

SPRING

All day the flicker
has anticipated
the lust of the season, by
shouting. He scouts up
tree after tree and at
a certain place begins
to cry out. My, in his
black-freckled vest, bay body with
red trim and sudden chrome
underwings, he is
dapper. Of course somebody
listening nearby
hears him; she answers
with a sound like hysterical
laughter, and rushes out into
the field where he is poised
on an old phone pole, his head
swinging, his wings
opening and shutting in a kind of
butterfly stroke. She can't
resist; they touch; they flutter.
How lightly, altogether, they accept
the great task, of carrying life
forward! In the crown of an oak
they choose a small tree-cave
which they enter with sudden quietness
and modesty. And, for a while,
the wind that can be
a knife or a hammer, subsides.

They listen
to the thrushes.
The sky is blue, or the rain
falls with its spills of pearl.
Around their wreath of darkness
the leaves of the world unfurl.

WHILE I AM WRITING A POEM TO CELEBRATE SUMMER, THE MEADOWLARK BEGINS TO SING

Sixty-seven years, oh Lord, to look at the clouds,
the trees in deep, moist summer,

daisies and morning glories
opening every morning

their small, ecstatic faces—
Or maybe I should just say

how I wish I had a voice
like the meadowlark's,

sweet, clear, and reliably
slurring all day long

from the fencepost, or the long grass
where it lives

in a tiny but adequate grass hut
beside the mullein and the everlasting,

the faint-pink roses
that have never been improved, but come to bud

then open like little soft sighs
under the meadowlark's whistle, its breath-praise,

its thrill-song, its anthem, its thanks, its
alleluia. Alleluia, oh Lord.

CATBIRD

He picks his pond, and the soft thicket of his world.
He bids his lady come, and she does,
    flirting with her tail.
He begins early, and makes up his song as he goes.
He does not enter a house at night, or when it rains.
He is not afraid of the wind, though he is cautious.
He watches the snake, that stripe of black fire,
    until it flows away.
He watches the hawk with her sharpest shins, aloft
    in the high tree.
He keeps his prayer under his tongue.
In his whole life he has never missed the rising of the sun.
He dislikes snow.
But a few raisins give him the greatest delight.
He sits in the forelock of the lilac, or he struts
    in its shadow.
He is neither the rare plover or the brilliant bunting,
    but as common as grass.
His black cap gives him a jaunty look, for which
    we humans have learned to tilt our caps, in envy.
When he is not singing, he is listening.
Neither have I ever seen him with his eyes closed.
Though he may be looking at nothing more than a cloud
    it brings to his mind a several dozen new remarks.
From one branch to another, or across the path,
    he dazzles with flight.
Since I see him every morning, I have rewarded myself
    the pleasure of thinking that he knows me.
Yet never, once has he answered my nod.

He seems, in fact, to find in me a kind of humor,
    I am so vast, uncertain and strange.
I am the one who comes and goes,
    and who knows why.
Will I ever understand him?
Certainly he will never understand me, or the world
    I come from.
For he will never sing for the kingdom of dollars.
For he will never grow pockets in his gray wings.

BACKYARD

I had no time to haul out all
the dead stuff so it hung, limp
or dry, wherever the wind swung it

over or down or across. All summer
it stayed that way, untrimmed, and
thickened. The paths grew
damp and uncomfortable and mossy until
nobody could get through but a mouse or a

shadow. Blackberries, ferns, leaves, litter
totally without direction management
supervision. The birds loved it.

FROM

What Do We Know?

2002

SUMMER POEM

Leaving the house,
I went out to see

the frog, for example,
in her shining green skin;

and her eggs
like a slippery veil;

and her eyes
with their golden rims;

and the pond
with its risen lilies;

and its warmed shores
dotted with pink flowers;

and the long, windless afternoon;
and the white heron

like a dropped cloud,
taking one slow step

then standing awhile then taking
another, writing

her own softfooted poem
through the still waters.

THE LOON

Not quite four a.m., when the rapture of being alive
strikes me from sleep, and I rise
from the comfortable bed and go
to another room, where my books are lined up
in their neat and colorful rows. How

magical they are! I choose one
and open it. Soon
I have wandered in over the waves of the words
to the temple of thought.

         And then I hear
outside, over the actual waves, the small,
perfect voice of the loon. He is also awake,
and with his heavy head uplifted he calls out
to the fading moon, to the pink flush
swelling in the east that, soon,
will become the long, reasonable day.

         Inside the house
it is still dark, except for the pool of lamplight
in which I am sitting.

         I do not close the book.

Neither, for a long while, do I read on.

WINTER AT HERRING COVE

Years ago,
in the bottle-green light
of the cold January sea,

two seals
suddenly appeared together
in a single uplifting wave—

each in exactly the same relaxed position—
each, like a large, black comma,
upright and staring;

it was like a painting
done twice
and, twice, tenderly.

The wave hung, then it broke apart;
its lip was lightning;
its floor was the blow of sand

over which the seals rose and twirled and were gone.
Of all the reasons for gladness,
what could be foremost of this one,

that the mind can seize both the instant and the memory!
Now the seals are no more than the salt of the sea.
If they live, they're more distant than Greenland.

. . .

But here's the kingdom we call remembrance
with its thousand iron doors
through which I pass so easily,

switching on the old lights as I go—
while the dead wind rises and the old rapture rewinds,
the stiff waters once more begin to kick and flow.

MINK

A mink,
     jointless as heat, was
tip-toeing along
     the edge of the creek,

which was still in its coat of snow,
     yet singing—I could hear it!—
the old song
     of brightness.

It was one of those places,
     turning and twisty,
that Ruskin might have painted, though
     he didn't. And there were trees
leaning this way and that,
     seed-beaded

buckthorn mostly, but at the moment
     no bird, the only voice
that of the covered water—like a long,
     unknotted thread, it kept
slipping through. The mink
     had a hunger in him

bigger than his shadow, which was gathered
     like a sheet of darkness under his
neat feet which were busy
     making dents in the snow. He sniffed
slowly and thoroughly in all
     four directions, as though

it was a prayer to the whole world, as far
    as he could capture its beautiful
smells—the iron of the air, the blood
    of necessity. Maybe, for him, even
the pink sun fading away to the edge
    of the world had a smell,

of roses, or of terror, who knows
    what his keen nose was
finding out. For me, it was the gift of the winter
    to see him. Once, like a hot, dark-brown pillar,
he stood up—and then he ran forward, and was gone.
    I stood awhile and then walked on

over the white snow: the terrible, gleaming
    loneliness. It took me, I suppose,
something like six more weeks to reach
    finally a patch of green, I paused so often
to be glad, and grateful, and even then carefully across
    the vast, deep woods I kept looking back.

BLUE IRIS

Now that I'm free to be myself, who am I?

Can't fly, can't run, and see how slowly I walk.

Well, I think, I can read books.

      "What's that you're doing?"
the green-headed fly shouts as it buzzes past.

I close the book.

Well, I can write down words, like these, softly.

"What's that you're doing?" whispers the wind, pausing
in a heap just outside the window.

Give me a little time, I say back to its staring, silver face.
It doesn't happen all of a sudden, you know.

"Doesn't it?" says the wind, and breaks open, releasing
distillation of blue iris.

And my heart panics not to be, as I long to be,
the empty, waiting, pure, speechless receptacle.

YOU ARE STANDING AT THE EDGE
OF THE WOODS

You are standing at the edge of the woods
at twilight
when something begins
to sing, like a waterfall

pouring down
through the leaves. It is
the thrush.
And you are just

sinking down into your thoughts,
taking in
the sweetness of it—those chords,
those pursed twirls—when you hear

out of the same twilight
the wildest red outcry. It pitches itself
forward, it flails and scabs
all the surrounding space with such authority

you can't tell
whether it is crying out on the
scarp of victory, with its hooked foot
dabbed into some creature that now

with snapped spine
lies on the earth—or whether
it is such a struck body itself, saying
goodbye.

The thrush
is silent then, or perhaps
has flown away.
The dark grows darker.

The moon,
in its shining white blouse,
rises.
And whatever that wild cry was

it will always remain a mystery
you have to go home now and live with,
sometimes with the ease of music, and sometimes in silence,
for the rest of your life.

THE ROSES

All afternoon I have been walking over the dunes,
hurrying from one thick raft of the wrinkled, salt
roses to another, leaning down close to their dark
or pale petals, red as blood or white as snow. And
now I am beginning to breathe slowly and evenly—
the way a hunted animal breathes, finally, when it
has galloped, and galloped—when it is wrung dry,
but, at last, is far away, so the panic begins to drain
from the chest, from the wonderful legs, and the
exhausted mind.

Oh sweetness pure and simple, may I join you?

I lie down next to them, on the sand. But to tell
about what happens next, truly I need help.

Will somebody or something please start to sing?

STONES

The white stones were mountains, then they went traveling.
The pink stones also were part of a mountain before
the glacier's tongue gathered them up.
Now they lie resting under the waves.
The green stones are lovelier than the blue stones, I thought
    for a little while,
then I changed my mind.
Stones born of the sediments tell what ooze floated down
    the outwash once.
Stones born of the fire have red stars inside their bodies,
    and seams of white quartz.
Also I admire the heft, and the circularities
as they lie without wrists or ankles just under the water.
Also I imagine how they lie quietly all night
under the moon and whatever passes overhead—say, the floating
    lily of the night-heron.
It is apparent also how they lie relaxed under the sun's
    golden ladders.
Each one is a slow-wheeler.
Each one is a tiny church, locked up tight.
Each one is perfect—but none of them is ready quite yet
to come to the garden, to raise corn
or the bulb of the iris.
If I lived inland I would want to take one or two home with me
just to look at in that long life of dust and grass,

but I hope I wouldn't.
I hope I wouldn't take even one like a seed from the sunflower's face,
like an ant's white egg from the warm nursery under the hill.
I hope I would leave them, in the perfect balance of things,
in the clear body of the sea.

ONE HUNDRED WHITE-SIDED DOLPHINS
ON A SUMMER DAY

1.

Fat,

black, slick,

galloping in the pitch

of the waves, in the pearly

fields of the sea,

they leap toward us,

they rise, sparkling, and vanish, and rise sparkling,

they breathe little clouds of mist, they lift perpetual smiles,

they slap their tails on the waves, grandmothers and grandfathers

enjoying the old jokes,

they circle around us,

they swim with us—

2.

a hundred white-sided dolphins

on a summer day,

each one, as God himself

could not appear more acceptable

a hundred times,

in a body blue and black threading through

the sea foam,

and lifting himself up from the opened

. . .

tents of the waves on his fishtail,
to look
with the moon of his eye
into my heart,

3.

and find there
pure, sudden, steep, sharp, painful
gratitude
that falls—

I don't know—either
unbearable tons
or the pale, bearable hand
of salvation

on my neck,
lifting me
from the boat's plain plank seat
into the world's

4.

unspeakable kindness.
It is my sixty-third summer on earth
and, for a moment, I have almost vanished
into the body of the dolphin,

into the moon-eye of God,
into the white fan that lies at the bottom of the sea
with everything
that ever was, or ever will be,

supple, wild, rising on flank or fishtail—
singing or whistling or breathing damply through blowhole
at top of head. Then, in our little boat, the dolphins suddenly gone,
we sailed on through the brisk, cheerful day.

The Leaf and
the Cloud

2000

FLARE

1.

Welcome to the silly, comforting poem.

It is not the sunrise,
which is a red rinse,
which is flaring all over the eastern sky;

it is not the rain falling out of the purse of God;

it is not the blue helmet of the sky afterward,

or the trees, or the beetle burrowing into the earth;

it is not the mockingbird who, in his own cadence,
will go on sizzling and clapping
from the branches of the catalpa that are thick with blossoms,
    that are billowing and shining,
        that are shaking in the wind.

2.

    You still recall, sometimes, the old barn on your great-grandfather's farm, a place you visited once, and went into, all alone, while the grownups sat and talked in the house.

    It was empty, or almost. Wisps of hay covered the floor, and some wasps sang at the windows, and maybe there was a strange fluttering bird high above, disturbed, hoo-ing a little and staring down from a messy ledge with wild, binocular eyes.

Mostly, though, it smelled of milk, and the patience of animals; the give-offs of the body were still in the air, a vague ammonia, not unpleasant.

Mostly, though, it was restful and secret, the roof high up and arched, the boards unpainted and plain.

You could have stayed there forever, a small child in a corner, on the last raft of hay, dazzled by so much space that seemed empty, but wasn't.

Then—you still remember—you felt the rap of hunger—it was noon—and you turned from that twilight dream and hurried back to the house, where the table was set, where an uncle patted you on the shoulder for welcome, and there was your place at the table.

3.

Nothing lasts.
There is a graveyard where everything I am talking about is,
now.

I stood there once, on the green grass, scattering flowers.

4.

Nothing is so delicate or so finely hinged as the wings
of the green moth
against the lantern
against its heat

against the beak of the crow
in the early morning.

Yet the moth has trim, and feistiness, and not a drop
    of self-pity.

Not in this world.

5.

My mother
was the blue wisteria,
my mother
was the mossy stream out behind the house,
my mother, *alas, alas,*
did not always love her life,
heavier than iron it was
as she carried it in her arms, from room to room,
oh, unforgettable!

I bury her
in a box
in the earth
and turn away.
My father
was a demon of frustrated dreams,
was a breaker of trust,
was a poor, thin boy with bad luck.
He followed God, there being no one else
he could talk to;

he swaggered before God, there being no one else
who would listen.
Listen,
this was his life.
I bury it in the earth.
I sweep the closets.
I leave the house.

6.

I mention them now,
I will not mention them again.

It is not lack of love
nor lack of sorrow.
But the iron thing they carried, I will not carry.

I give them—one, two, three, four—the kiss of courtesy,
    of sweet thanks,
of anger, of good luck in the deep earth.
May they sleep well. May they soften.

But I will not give them the kiss of complicity.
I will not give them the responsibility for my life.

7.

Did you know that the ant has a tongue
with which to gather in all that it can
of sweetness?

. . .

Did you know that?

8.

The poem is not the world.
It isn't even the first page of the world.

But the poem wants to flower, like a flower.
It knows that much.

It wants to open itself,
like the door of a little temple,
so that you might step inside and be cooled and refreshed,
and less yourself than part of everything.

9.

The voice of the child crying out of the mouth of the
    grown woman
is a misery and a disappointment.
The voice of the child howling out of the tall, bearded,
    muscular man
is a misery, and a terror.

10.

Therefore, tell me:
what will engage you?
What will open the dark fields of your mind,
    like a lover
        at first touching?

11.

Anyway,
there was no barn.
No child in the barn.

No uncle no table no kitchen.

Only a long lovely field full of bobolinks.

12.

When loneliness comes stalking, go into the fields, consider
the orderliness of the world. Notice
something you have never noticed before,

like the tambourine sound of the snow-cricket
whose pale green body is no longer than your thumb.

Stare hard at the hummingbird, in the summer rain,
shaking the water-sparks from its wings.

Let grief be your sister, she will whether or no.
Rise up from the stump of sorrow, and be green also,
    like the diligent leaves.

A lifetime isn't long enough for the beauty of this world
and the responsibilities of your life.

Scatter your flowers over the graves, and walk away.
Be good-natured and untidy in your exuberance.

. . .

In the glare of your mind, be modest.
And beholden to what is tactile, and thrilling.

Live with the beetle, and the wind.

This is the dark bread of the poem.
This is the dark and nourishing bread of the poem.

FROM THE BOOK OF TIME

1.

I rose this morning early as usual, and went to my desk.
But it's spring,

and the thrush is in the woods,
somewhere in the twirled branches, and he is singing.

And so, now, I am standing by the open door.
And now I am stepping down onto the grass.

I am touching a few leaves.
I am noticing the way the yellow butterflies
move together, in a twinkling cloud, over the field.

And I am thinking: maybe just looking and listening
is the real work.

Maybe the world, without us,
is the real poem.

2.

For how many years have you gone through the house
     shutting the windows,
while the rain was still five miles away

and veering, o plum-colored clouds, to the north,
away from you

and you did not even know enough
to be sorry,

you were glad
those silver sheets, with the occasional golden staple,

were sweeping on, elsewhere,
violent and electric and uncontrollable—

and will you find yourself finally wanting to forget
all enclosures, including

the enclosure of yourself, o lonely leaf, and will you
dash finally, frantically,

to the windows and haul them open and lean out
to the dark, silvered sky, to everything

that is beyond capture, shouting
I'm here, I'm here! Now, now, now, now, now.

3.

I dreamed
I was traveling
from one country
to another

jogging
on the back
of a white horse
whose hooves

. . .

were the music
of dust and gravel
whose halter
was made of the leafy braids

of flowers,
whose name
was Earth.
And it never

grew tired
though the sun
went down
like a thousand roses

and the stars
put their white faces
in front of the black branches
above us

and then
there was nothing around us
but water
and the white horse

turned suddenly
like a bolt of white cloth
opening
under the cloth-cutter's deft hands

. . .

and became
a swan.
Its red tongue
flickered out

as it perceived
my great surprise
my huge and unruly pleasure
my almost unmanageable relief. . . .

4.

"'Whoever shall be guided so far towards the mysteries of love, by
contemplating beautiful things rightly in due order, is approaching the
last grade. Suddenly he will behold a beauty marvellous in its nature,
that very Beauty, Socrates, for the sake of which all the earlier
hardships had been borne: in the first place, everlasting, and never
being born nor perishing, neither increasing nor diminishing;
secondly, not beautiful here and ugly there, not beautiful now and ugly
then, not beautiful in one direction and ugly in another direction, not
beautiful in one place and ugly in another place. Again, this beauty
will not show itself like a face or hands or any bodily thing at all, nor
as a discourse or a science, nor indeed as residing in anything, as in a
living creature or in earth or heaven or anything else, but being by
itself with itself always in simplicity; while all the beautiful things
elsewhere partake of this beauty in such manner, that when *they* are
born and perish *it* becomes neither less nor more and nothing at all
happens to it. . . .'"

5.

What secrets fly out of the earth
when I push the shovel-edge,
when I heave the dirt open?

And if there are no secrets
what is that smell that sweetness rising?

What is my name,
o what is my name
that I may offer it back
to the beautiful world?

Have I walked
long enough
where the sea breaks raspingly
all day and all night upon the pale sand?

Have I admired sufficiently the little hurricane
of the hummingbird?

the heavy
thumb
of the blackberry?

the falling star?

6.

Count the roses, red and fluttering.
Count the roses, wrinkled and salt.
Each with its yellow lint at the center.
Each with its honey pooled and ready.
Do you have a question that can't be answered?
Do the stars frighten you by their heaviness
    and their endless number?
Does it bother you, that mercy is so difficult to
    understand?
For some souls it's easy; they lie down on the sand
    and are soon asleep.
For others, the mind shivers in its glacial palace,
    and won't come.
Yes, the mind takes a long time, is otherwise occupied
than by happiness, and deep breathing.
Now, in the distance, some bird is singing.
And now I have gathered six or seven deep red,
    half-opened cups of petals between my hands,
and now I have put my face against them
and now I am moving my face back and forth, slowly,
    against them.
The body is not much more than two feet and a tongue.
Come to me, says the blue sky, and say the word.
And finally even the mind comes running, like a wild thing,
    and lies down in the sand.
Eternity is not later, or in any unfindable place.
Roses, roses, roses, roses.

7.

Even now
I remember something

the way a flower
in a jar of water

remembers its life
in the perfect garden

the way a flower
in a jar of water

remembers its life
as a closed seed

the way a flower
in a jar of water

steadies itself
remembering itself

long ago
the plunging roots

the gravel the rain
the glossy stem

the wings of the leaves
the swords of the leaves

. . .

rising and clashing
for the rose of the sun

the salt of the stars
the crown of the wind

the beds of the clouds
the blue dream

the unbreakable circle.

FROM

West Wind

1997

HAVE YOU EVER TRIED TO ENTER
THE LONG BLACK BRANCHES

Have you ever tried to enter the long black branches
    of other lives—
tried to imagine what the crisp fringes, full of honey,
    hanging
from the branches of the young locust trees, in early summer,
    feel like?

Do you think this world is only an entertainment for you?

Never to enter the sea and notice how the water divides
    with perfect courtesy, to let you in!
Never to lie down on the grass, as though you were the grass!
Never to leap to the air as you open your wings over
    the dark acorn of your heart!

No wonder we hear, in your mournful voice, the complaint
    that something is missing from your life!

Who can open the door who does not reach for the latch?
Who can travel the miles who does not put one foot
    in front of the other, all attentive to what presents itself
    continually?
Who will behold the inner chamber who has not observed
    with admiration, even with rapture, the outer stone?

Well, there is time left—
fields everywhere invite you into them.

. . .

And who will care, who will chide you if you wander away
    from wherever you are, to look for your soul?

Quickly, then, get up, put on your coat, leave your desk!

To put one's foot into the door of the grass, which is
    the mystery, which is death as well as life, and
    not be afraid!

To set one's foot in the door of death, and be overcome
    with amazement!

To sit down in front of the weeds, and imagine
    god the ten-fingered, sailing out of his house of straw,

nodding this way and that way, to the flowers of the
    present hour,

to the song falling out of the mockingbird's pink mouth,

to the tiplets of the honeysuckle, that have opened
    in the night

To sit down, like a weed among weeds, and rustle in the wind!

—◦◦◦—

Listen, are you breathing just a little, and calling it a life?

. . .

While the soul, after all, is only a window,
and the opening of the window no more difficult
than the wakening from a little sleep.

——∞——

Only last week I went out among the thorns and said
    to the wild roses:
deny me not,
but suffer my devotion.
Then, all afternoon, I sat among them. Maybe

I even heard a curl or two of music, damp and rouge red,
hurrying from their stubby buds, from their delicate watery bodies.

——∞——

For how long will you continue to listen to those dark shouters,
    caution and prudence?

Fall in! Fall in!

——∞——

A woman standing in the weeds.
A small boat flounders in the deep waves, and what's coming next
    is coming with its own heave and grace.

——∞——

Meanwhile, once in a while, I have chanced, among the quick things,
    upon the immutable.
What more could one ask?

. . .

And I would touch the faces of the daises,
and I would bow down
to think about it.

That was then, which hasn't ended yet.

Now the sun begins to swing down. Under the peach-light,
I cross the fields and the dunes, I follow the ocean's edge.

I climb, I backtrack.
I float.
I ramble my way home.

SEVEN WHITE BUTTERFLIES

Seven white butterflies
delicate in a hurry look
how they bang the pages
    of their wings as they fly

to the fields of mustard yellow
and orange and plain
gold all eternity
    is in the moment this is what

Blake said Whitman said such
wisdom in the agitated
motions of the mind seven
    dancers floating

even as worms toward
paradise see how they banter
and riot and rise
    to the trees flutter

lob their white bodies into
the invisible wind weightless
lacy willing
    to deliver themselves unto

. . .

the universe now each settles
down on a yellow thumb on a
brassy stem now
　　all seven are rapidly sipping

from the golden towers who
would have thought it could be so easy?

AT ROUND POND

owl
make your little appearance now   ,

owl dark bird bird of gloom
messenger reminder

of death
that can't be stopped

argued with leashed put out
like a red fire but

burns as it will
owl

I have not seen you now for
too long a time don't

hide away but come flowing and clacking
the slap of your wings

your death's head oh rise
out of the thick and shaggy pines when you

look down with your
golden eyes how everything

. . .

trembles
then settles

from mere incidence into
the lush of meaning.

BLACK OAKS

Okay, not one can write a symphony, or a dictionary,
    or even a letter to an old friend, full of remembrance
    and comfort.

Not one can manage a single sound, though the blue jays
    carp and whistle all day in the branches, without
    the push of the wind.

But to tell the truth after a while I'm pale with longing
    for their thick bodies ruckled with lichen

and you can't keep me from the woods, from the tonnage
    of their shoulders, and their shining green hair.

Today is a day like any other: twenty-four hours, a
    little sunshine, a little rain.

Listen, says ambition, nervously shifting her weight from
    one boot to another—why don't you get going?

For there I am, in the mossy shadows, under the trees.

And to tell the truth I don't want to let go of the wrists
    of idleness, I don't want to sell my life for money,
    I don't even want to come in out of the rain.

AM I NOT AMONG THE EARLY RISERS

Am I not among the early risers
and the long-distance walkers?

Have I not stood, amazed, as I consider
the perfection of the morning star
above the peaks of the houses, and the crowns of the trees
    blue in the first light?
Do I not see how the trees tremble, as though
    sheets of water flowed over them
though it is only wind, that common thing,
    free to everyone, and everything?

Have I not thought, for years, what it would be
worthy to do, and then gone off, barefoot and with a silver pail,
    to gather blueberries,
thus coming, as I think, upon a right answer?

What will ambition do for me that the fox, appearing suddenly
at the top of the field,
her eyes sharp and confident as she stared into mine,
has not already done?

What countries, what visitations,
    what pomp
would satisfy me as thoroughly as Blackwater Woods
on a sun-filled morning, or, equally, in the rain?

Here is an amazement—once I was twenty years old and in
    every motion of my body there was a delicious ease,

and in every motion of the green earth there was
  a hint of paradise,
and now I am sixty years old, and it is the same.

Above the modest house and the palace—the same darkness.
Above the evil man and the just, the same stars.
Above the child who will recover and the child who will
  not recover, the same energies roll forward,
from one tragedy to the next and from one foolishness to the next.

  I bow down.

Have I not loved as though the beloved could vanish at any moment,
or become preoccupied, or whisper a name other than mine
  in the stretched curvatures of lust, or over the dinner table?
Have I ever taken good fortune for granted?

Have I not, every spring, befriended the swarm that pours forth?
Have I not summoned the honey-man to come, to hurry,
  to bring with him the white and comfortable hive?

And, while I waited, have I not leaned close, to see everything?
Have I not been stung as I watched their milling and gleaming,
  and stung hard?

Have I not been ready always at the iron door,
  not knowing to what country it opens—to death or to more life?

Have I ever said that the day was too hot or too cold
or the night too long and as black as oil anyway,
or the morning, washed blue and emptied entirely
 of the second-rate, less than happiness

as I stepped down from the porch and set out along
the green paths of the world?

FOX

You don't ever know where
a sentence will take you, depending
on its roll and fold. I was walking
over the dunes when I saw
the red fox asleep under the green
branches of the pine. It flared up
in the sweet order of its being,
the tail that was over the muzzle
lifting in airy amazement
and the fire of the eyes followed
and the pricked ears and the thin
barrel body and the four
athletic legs in their black stockings and it
came to me how the polish of the world changes
everything, I was hot I was cold I was almost
dead of delight. Of course the mind keeps
cool in its hidden palace—yes, the mind takes
a long time, is otherwise occupied than by
happiness, and deep breathing. Still,
at last, it comes too, running
like a wild thing, to be taken
with its twin sister, breath. So I stood
on the pale, peach-colored sand, watching the fox
as it opened like a flower, and I began
softly, to pick among the vast assortment of words
that it should run again and again across the page
that you again and again should shiver with praise.

FROM "WEST WIND"

1.

If there is life after the earth-life, will you come with me?
Even then? Since we're bound to be something, why not
together. Imagine! Two little stones, two fleas under the
wing of a gull, flying along through the fog! Or, ten blades
of grass. Ten loops of honeysuckle, all flung against each
other, at the edge of Race Road! Beach plums! Snowflakes,
coasting into the winter woods, making a very small sound,
like this

soooooooooooooooooooooooooooooooooooooooooooooo

as they marry the dusty bodies of the pitch-pines. Or, rain—
that gray light running over the sea, pocking it, lacquering
it, coming, all morning and afternoon, from the west wind's
youth and abundance and jollity—pinging and jangling
down upon the roofs of Provincetown.

9.

And what did you think love would be like?
A summer day? The brambles in their places,
and the long stretches of mud? Flowers in every
field, in every garden, with their soft beaks and
their pastel shoulders? On one street after another,
the litter ticks in the gutter. In one room
after another, the lovers meet, quarrel, sicken,
break apart, cry out. One or two leap from
windows. Most simply lean, exhausted, their
thin arms on the sill. They have done all that
they could. The golden eagle, that lives not far
from here, has perhaps a thousand tiny feathers
flowing from the back of its head, each one shaped
like an infinitely small but perfect spear.

FROM

White Pine

1994

MAY

What lay on the road was no mere handful of snake. It was the copperhead at last, golden under the street lamp. I hope to see everything in this world before I die. I knelt on the road and stared. Its head was wedge-shaped and fell back to the unexpected slimness of a neck. The body itself was thick, tense, electric. Clearly this wasn't black snake looking down from the limbs of a tree, or green snake, or the garter, whizzing over the rocks. Where these had, oh, such shyness, this one had none. When I moved a little, it turned and clamped its eyes on mine; then it jerked toward me. I jumped back and watched as it flowed on across the road and down into the dark. My heart was pounding. I stood a while, listening to the small sounds of the woods and looking at the stars. After excitement we are so restful. When the thumb of fear lifts, we are so alive.

YES! NO!

How necessary it is to have opinions! I think the spotted trout lilies are satisfied, standing a few inches above the earth. I think serenity is not something you just find in the world, like a plum tree, holding up its white petals.

The violets, along the river, are opening their blue faces, like small dark lanterns.

The green mosses, being so many, are as good as brawny.

How important it is to walk along, not in haste but slowly, looking at everything and calling out

Yes! No! The

swan, for all his pomp, his robes of glass and petals, wants only to be allowed to live on the nameless pond. The catbrier is without fault. The water thrushes, down among the sloppy rocks, are going crazy with happiness. Imagination is better than a sharp instrument. To pay attention, this is our endless and proper work.

IN POBIDDY, GEORGIA

Three women
climb from the car
in which they have driven slowly
into the churchyard.
They come toward us, to see
what we are doing.
What we are doing
is reading the strange,
wonderful names
of the dead.
One of the women
speaks to us—
after we speak to her.
She walks with us and shows us,
with a downward-thrust finger,
which of the dead
were her people.
She tells us
about two brothers, and an argument,
and a gun—she points
to one of the slabs
on which there is a name,
some scripture, a handful of red
plastic flowers. We ask her
about the other brother.
"Chain gang," she says,
as you or I might say
"Des Moines," or "New Haven." And then,
"Look around all you want."

The younger woman stands back, in the stiff weeds,
like a banked fire.
The third one—
the oldest human being we have ever seen in our lives—
suddenly drops to the dirt
and begins to cry. Clearly
she is blind, and clearly
she can't rise, but they lift her, like a child,
and lead her away, across the graves, as though,
as old as anything could ever be, she was, finally,
perfectly finished, perfectly heartbroken, perfectly wild.

PORCUPINE

Where
the porcupine is
I don't
know but I hope

it's high
up on some pine
bough in some
thick tree, maybe

on the other side
of the swamp.
The dogs have come
running back, one of them

with a single quill
in his moist nose.
He's laughing,
not knowing what he has

almost done
to himself.
For years I have wanted to see
that slow rambler,

that thornbush.
I think, what love does to us
is a Gordian knot,
it's that complicated.

I hug the dogs
and their good luck,
and put on their leashes.
So dazzling she must be—

a plump, dark lady
wearing a gown of nails —
white teeth tearing skin
from the thick tree.

WRENS

here I go
into the wide gardens of
wastefields blue glass clear glass
and other rubbishes blinking from the

dust from the fox tracks among the
roots and risings of
buttercups joe pye honey

suckle the queen's
lace and her

blue sailors

the little wrens
have carried a hundred sticks into

an old rusted pail and now they are
singing in the curtains of leaves they are

fluttering down to the bog they are dipping

their darling heads down to wet

their whistles how happy they are to be
diligent at last

foolish birds

MOCKINGBIRDS

This morning
two mockingbirds
in the green field
were spinning and tossing

the white ribbons
of their songs
into the air.
I had nothing

better to do
than listen.
I mean this
seriously.

In Greece,
a long time ago,
an old couple
opened their door

to two strangers
who were,
it soon appeared,
not men at all,

but gods.
It is my favorite story—
how the old couple
had almost nothing to give

but their willingness
to be attentive—
and for this alone
the gods loved them

and blessed them.
When the gods rose
out of their mortal bodies,
like a million particles of water

from a fountain,
the light
swept into all the corners
of the cottage,

and the old couple,
shaken with understanding,
bowed down—
but still they asked for nothing

beyond the difficult life
which they had already.
And the gods smiled as they vanished,
clapping their great wings.

Wherever it was
I was supposed to be
this morning—
whatever it was I said

I would be doing—
I was standing
at the edge of the field—
I was hurrying

through my own soul,
opening its dark doors—
I was leaning out;
I was listening.

I FOUND A DEAD FOX

I found a dead fox
beside the gravel road,
curled inside the big
iron wheel

of an old tractor
that has been standing,
for years,
in the vines at the edge

of the road.
I don't know
what happened to it—
when it came there

or why it lay down
for good, settling
its narrow chin
on the rusted rim

of the iron wheel
to look out
over the fields,
and that way died—

but I know
this: its posture—
of looking,
to the last possible moment,

back into the world—
made me want
to sing something
joyous and tender

about foxes.
But what happened is this—
when I began,
when I crawled in

through the honeysuckle
and lay down,
curling my long spine
inside that cold wheel,

and touched the dead fox,
and looked out
into the wide fields,
the fox

vanished.
There was only myself
and the world,
and it was I

who was leaving.
And what could I sing
then?
Oh, beautiful world!

I just lay there
and looked at it.
And then it grew dark.
That day was done with.

And then the stars stepped forth
and held up their appointed fires—
those hot, hard
watchmen of the night.

MORNING GLORIES

Blue and dark-blue
   rose and deepest rose
      white and pink they

are everywhere in the diligent
   cornfield rising and swaying
      in their reliable

finery in the little
   fling of their bodies their
      gear and tackle

all caught up in the cornstalks.
   The reaper's story is the story
      of endless work of

work careful and heavy but the
   reaper cannot
      separate them out there they

are in the story of his life
   bright random useless
      year after year

taken with the serious tons
   weeds without value humorous
      beautiful weeds.

AUGUST

Our neighbor, tall and blond and vigorous, the mother of many children, is sick. We did not know she was sick, but she has come to the fence, walking like a woman who is balancing a sword inside of her body, and besides that her long hair is gone, it is short and, suddenly, gray. I don't recognize her. It even occurs to me that it might be her mother. But it's her own laughter-edged voice, we have heard it for years over the hedges.

All summer the children, grown now and some of them with children of their own, come to visit. They swim, they go for long walks along the harbor, they make dinners for twelve, for fifteen, for twenty. In the early morning two daughters come to the garden and slowly go through the precise and silent gestures of T'ai Chi.

They all smile. Their father smiles too, and builds castles on the shore with the children, and drives back to the city, and drives back to the country. A carpenter is hired—a roof repaired, a porch rebuilt. Everything that can be fixed.

June, July, August. Every day, we hear their laughter. I think of the painting by van Gogh, the man in the chair. Everything wrong, and nowhere to go. His hands over his eyes.

TOAD

I was walking by. He was sitting there.

It was full morning, so the heat was heavy on his sand-colored head and his webbed feet. I squatted beside him, at the edge of the path. He didn't move.

I began to talk. I talked about summer, and about time. The pleasures of eating, the terrors of the night. About this cup we call a life. About happiness. And how good it feels, the heat of the sun between the shoulder blades.

He looked neither up nor down, which didn't necessarily mean he was either afraid or asleep. I felt his energy, stored under his tongue perhaps, and behind his bulging eyes.

I talked about how the world seems to me, five feet tall, the blue sky all around my head. I said, I wondered how it seemed to him, down there, intimate with the dust.

He might have been Buddha—did not move, blink, or frown, not a tear fell from those gold-rimmed eyes as the refined anguish of language passed over him.

I LOOKED UP

I looked up and there it was
among the green branches of the pitchpines—

thick bird,
a ruffle of fire trailing over the shoulders and down the back—

color of copper, iron, bronze—
lighting up the dark branches of the pine.

What misery to be afraid of death.
What wretchedness, to believe only in what can be proven.

When I made a little sound
it looked at me, then it looked past me.

Then it rose, the wings enormous and opulent,
and, as I said, wreathed in fire.

THE SEA MOUSE

What lay this morning
on the wet sand
was so ugly
I sighed with a kind of horror as I lifted it

into my hand
and looked under the soaked mat of what was almost fur,
but wasn't, and found
the face that has no eyes, and recognized

the sea mouse—
toothless, legless, earless too,
it had been flung out of the stormy sea
and dropped

into the world's outer weather, and clearly it was
done for. I studied
what was not even a fist
of gray corduroy;

I looked in vain
for elbows and wrists;
I counted
the thirty segments, with which

.   .   .

it had rippled its mouse-like dance
over the sea's black floor—not on
feet, which it did not have, but on
tiny buds tipped with bristles,

like paintbrushes—
to find and swallow
the least pulse, and so stay alive, and feel—
however a worm feels it—satisfaction.

Before me
the sea still heaved, and the heavens were dark,
the storm unfinished,
and whatever was still alive

stirred in the awful cup of its power,
though it breathe like fire, though it love
the lung of its own life.
Little mat, little blot, little crawler,

it lay in my hand
all delicate and revolting.
With the tip of my finger
I stroked it,

. . .

tenderly, little darling, little dancer,
little pilgrim,
gray pouch slowly
filling with death.

FROM

New and
Selected Poems:
Volume One

1992

THE SUN

Have you ever seen
anything
in your life
more wonderful

than the way the sun,
every evening,
relaxed and easy,
floats toward the horizon

and into the clouds or the hills,
or the rumpled sea,
and is gone—
and how it slides again

out of the blackness,
every morning,
on the other side of the world,
like a red flower

streaming upward on its heavenly oils,
say, on a morning in early summer,
at its perfect imperial distance—
and have you ever felt for anything

such wild love—
do you think there is anywhere, in any language,
a word billowing enough
for the pleasure

. . .

that fills you,
as the sun
reaches out,
as it warms you

as you stand there,
empty-handed—
or have you too
turned from this world—

or have you too
gone crazy
for power,
for things?

GOLDENROD

On roadsides,
   in fall fields,
      in rumpy bunches,
         saffron and orange and pale gold,

in little towers,
   soft as mash,
      sneeze-bringers and seed-bearers,
         full of bees and yellow beads and perfect flowerlets

and orange butterflies.
   I don't suppose
      much notice comes of it, except for honey,
         and how it heartens the heart with its

blank blaze.
   I don't suppose anything loves it except, perhaps,
      the rocky voids
         filled by its dumb dazzle.

For myself,
   I was just passing by, when the wind flared
      and the blossoms rustled,
         and the glittering pandemonium

leaned on me.
   I was just minding my own business
      when I found myself on their straw hillsides,
         citron and butter-colored,

. . .

and was happy, and why not?
  Are not the difficult labors of our lives
    full of dark hours?
      And what has consciousness come to anyway, so far,

that is better than these light-filled bodies?
  All day
    on their airy backbones
      they toss in the wind,

they bend as though it was natural and godly to bend,
  they rise in a stiff sweetness,
    in the pure peace of giving
      one's gold away.

WHEN DEATH COMES

When death comes
like the hungry bear in autumn;
when death comes and takes all the bright coins from his purse

to buy me, and snaps the purse shut;
when death comes
like the measle-pox;

when death comes
like an iceberg between the shoulder blades,

I want to step through the door full of curiosity, wondering:
what is it going to be like, that cottage of darkness?

And therefore I look upon everything
as a brotherhood and a sisterhood,
and I look upon time as no more than an idea,
and I consider eternity as another possibility,

and I think of each life as a flower, as common
as a field daisy, and as singular,

and each name a comfortable music in the mouth,
tending, as all music does, toward silence,

and each body a lion of courage, and something
precious to the earth.

When it's over, I want to say: all my life
I was a bride married to amazement.
I was the bridegroom, taking the world into my arms.

. . .

When it's over, I don't want to wonder
if I have made of my life something particular, and real.
I don't want to find myself sighing and frightened,
or full of argument.

I don't want to end up simply having visited this world.

WHELKS

Here are the perfect
fans of the scallops,
quahogs, and weedy mussels
still holding their orange fruit—
and here are the whelks—
whirlwinds,
each the size of a fist,
but always cracked and broken—
clearly they have been traveling
under the sky-blue waves
for a long time.
All my life
I have been restless—
I have felt there is something
more wonderful than gloss—
than wholeness—
than staying at home.
I have not been sure what it is.
But every morning on the wide shore
I pass what is perfect and shining
to look for the whelks, whose edges
have rubbed so long against the world
they have snapped and crumbled—
they have almost vanished,
with the last relinquishing
of their unrepeatable energy,
back into everything else.
When I find one
I hold it in my hand,

I look out over that shanking fire,
I shut my eyes. Not often,
but now and again there's a moment
when the heart cries aloud:
yes, I am willing to be
that wild darkness,
that long, blue body of light.

GOLDFINCHES

In the fields
we let them have—
in the fields
we don't want yet—

where thistles rise
out of the marshlands of spring, and spring open—
each bud
a settlement of riches—

a coin of reddish fire—
the finches
wait for midsummer,
for the long days,

for the brass heat,
for the seeds to begin to form in the hardening thistles,
dazzling as the teeth of mice,
but black,

filling the face of every flower.
Then they drop from the sky.
A buttery gold,
they swing on the thistles, they gather

the silvery down, they carry it
in their finchy beaks
to the edges of the fields,
to the trees,

as though their minds were on fire

with the flower of one perfect idea—
and there they build their nests
and lay their pale-blue eggs,

every year,
and every year
the hatchlings wake in the swaying branches
in the silver baskets,

and love the world.
Is it necessary to say any more?
Have you heard them singing in the wind, above the final fields?
Have you ever been so happy in your life?

POPPIES

The poppies send up their
orange flares; swaying
in the wind, their congregations
are a levitation

of bright dust, of thin
and lacy leaves.
There isn't a place
in this world that doesn't

sooner or later drown
in the indigos of darkness,
but now, for a while,
the roughage

shines like a miracle
as it floats above everything
with its yellow hair.
Of course nothing stops the cold,

black, curved blade
from hooking forward—
of course
loss is the great lesson.

But also I say this: that light
is an invitation
to happiness,
and that happiness,

. . .

when it's done right,
is a kind of holiness,
palpable and redemptive.
Inside the bright fields,

touched by their rough and spongy gold,
I am washed and washed
in the river
of earthly delight—

and what are you going to do—
what can you do
about it—
deep, blue night?

WATER SNAKE

I saw him
in a dry place
on a hot day,
a traveler
making his way
from one pond
to another,
and he lifted up
his chary face
and looked at me
with his gravel eyes,
and the feather of his tongue
shot in and out
of his otherwise clamped mouth,
and I stopped on the path
to give him room,
and he went past me
with his head high,
loathing me, I think,
for my long legs,
my poor body, like a post,
my many fingers,
for he didn't linger
but, touching the other side of the path,
he headed, in long lunges and quick heaves,
straight to the nearest basin
of sweet black water and weeds,
and solitude—

like an old sword
that suddenly picked itself up and went off,
swinging, swinging
through the green leaves.

WHITE FLOWERS

Last night
in the fields
I lay down in the darkness
to think about death,
but instead I fell asleep,
as if in a vast and sloping room
filled with those white flowers
that open all summer,
sticky and untidy,
in the warm fields.
When I woke
the morning light was just slipping
in front of the stars,
and I was covered
with blossoms.
I don't know
how it happened—
I don't know
if my body went diving down
under the sugary vines
in some sleep-sharpened affinity
with the depths, or whether
that green energy
rose like a wave
and curled over me, claiming me
in its husky arms.
I pushed them away, but I didn't rise.
Never in my life had I felt so plush,
or so slippery,

or so resplendently empty.
Never in my life
had I felt myself so near
that porous line
where my own body was done with
and the roots and the stems and the flowers
began.

PEONIES

This morning the green fists of the peonies are getting ready
    to break my heart
        as the sun rises,
            as the sun strokes them with his old, buttery fingers

and they open—
    pools of lace,
        white and pink—
            and all day the black ants climb over them,

boring their deep and mysterious holes
    into the curls,
        craving the sweet sap,
            taking it away

to their dark, underground cities—
    and all day
        under the shifty wind,
            as in a dance to the great wedding,

the flowers bend their bright bodies,
    and tip their fragrance to the air,
        and rise,
            their red stems holding

all that dampness and recklessness
    gladly and lightly,
        and there it is again—
            beauty the brave, the exemplary,

blazing open.
    Do you love this world?
        Do you cherish your humble and silky life?
            Do you adore the green grass, with its terror beneath?

Do you also hurry, half-dressed and barefoot, into the garden,
    and softly,
        and exclaiming of their dearness,
            fill your arms with the white and pink flowers,

with their honeyed heaviness, their lush trembling,
    their eagerness
        to be wild and perfect for a moment, before they are
            nothing, forever?

THE EGRET

Every time
but one
the little fish
and the green
and spotted frogs
know
the egret's bamboo legs
from the thin
and polished reeds
at the edge
of the silky world
of water.
Then,
in their last inch of time,
they see,
for an instant,
the white froth
of her shoulders,

and the white scrolls
of her belly,
and the white flame
of her head.
What more can you say
about such wild swimmers?
They were here,
they were silent,
they are gone, having tasted
sheer terror.
Therefore I have invented words
with which to stand back
on the weedy shore—
with which to say:
Look! Look!
What is this dark death
that opens
like a white door?

RICE

It grew in the black mud.
It grew under the tiger's orange paws.
Its stems thinner than candles, and as straight.
Its leaves like the feathers of egrets, but green.
The grains cresting, wanting to burst.
Oh, blood of the tiger.

I don't want you just to sit down at the table.
I don't want you just to eat, and be content.
I want you to walk out into the fields
where the water is shining, and the rice has risen.
I want you to stand there, far from the white tablecloth.
I want you to fill your hands with the mud, like a blessing.

RAIN

1.

All afternoon it rained, then
such power came down from the clouds
on a yellow thread,
as authoritative as God is supposed to be.
When it hit the tree, her body
opened forever.

2. The Swamp

Last night, in the rain, some of the men climbed over
    the barbed-wire fence of the detention center.
In the darkness they wondered if they could do it, and knew
    they had to try to do it.
In the darkness they climbed the wire, handful after handful
    of barbed wire.
Even in the darkness most of them were caught and sent back
    to the camp inside.
But a few are still climbing the barbed wire, or wading through
    the blue swamp on the other side.

What does barbed wire feel like when you grip it, as though
    it were a loaf of bread, or a pair of shoes?
What does barbed wire feel like when you grip it, as though
    it were a plate and a fork, or a handful of flowers?
What does barbed wire feel like when you grip it, as though
    it were the handle of a door, working papers, a clean sheet
    you want to draw over your body?

3.

Or this one: on a rainy day, my uncle
lying in the flower bed,
cold and broken,
dragged from the idling car
with its plug of rags, and its gleaming
length of hose. My father
shouted,
then the ambulance came,
then we all looked at death,
then the ambulance took him away.
From the porch of the house
I turned back once again
looking for my father, who had lingered,
who was still standing in the flowers,
who was that motionless muddy man,
who was that tiny figure in the rain.

4. Early Morning, My Birthday

The snails on the pink sleds of their bodies are moving
    among the morning glories.
The spider is asleep among the red thumbs
    of the raspberries.
What shall I do, what shall I do?

The rain is slow.
The little birds are alive in it.
Even the beetles.

The green leaves lap it up.
What shall I do, what shall I do?

The wasp sits on the porch of her paper castle.
The blue heron floats out of the clouds.
The fish leap, all rainbow and mouth, from the dark water.

This morning the water lilies are no less lovely, I think,
    than the lilies of Monet.
And I do not want anymore to be useful, to be docile, to lead
children out of the fields into the text
of civility to teach them that they are (they are not) better
    than the grass.

5. At the Edge of the Ocean

I have heard this music before,
saith the body.

6. The Garden

The kale's
puckered sleeve,
the pepper's
hollow bell,
the lacquered onion.

Beets, borage, tomatoes.
Green beans.

. . .

I came in and I put everything
on the counter: chives, parsley, dill,
the squash like a pale moon,
peas in their silky shoes, the dazzling
rain-drenched corn.

7. The Forest

At night
under the trees
the black snake
jellies forward
rubbing
roughly
the stems of the bloodroot,
the yellow leaves,
little boulders of bark,
to take off
the old life.
I don't know
if he knows
what is happening.
I don't know
if he knows
it will work.
In the distance
the moon and the stars
give a little light.
In the distance
the owl cries out.

. . .

In the distance
the owl cries out.
The snake knows
these are the owl's woods,
these are the woods of death,
these are the woods of hardship
where you crawl and crawl,
where you live in the husks of trees,
where you lie on the wild twigs
and they cannot bear your weight,
where life has no purpose
and is neither civil nor intelligent.

Where life has no purpose,
and is neither civil nor intelligent,
it begins
to rain,
it begins
to smell like the bodies
of flowers.
At the back of the neck
the old skin splits.
The snake shivers
but does not hesitate.
He inches forward.
He begins to bleed through
like satin.

PICKING BLUEBERRIES,
AUSTERLITZ, NEW YORK, 1957

Once, in summer,
　in the blueberries,
　　I fell asleep, and woke
　　　when a deer stumbled against me.

I guess
　she was so busy with her own happiness
　　she had grown careless
　　　and was just wandering along

listening
　to the wind as she leaned down
　　to lip up the sweetness.
　　　So, there we were

with nothing between us
　but a few leaves, and the wind's
　　glossy voice
　　　shouting instructions.

The deer
　backed away finally
　　and flung up her white tail
　　　and went floating off toward the trees—

but the moment before she did that
　was so wide and so deep
　　it has lasted to this day;
　　　I have only to think of her—

. . .

the flower of her amazement
    and the stalled breath of her curiosity,
        and even the damp touch of her solicitude
           before she took flight—

to be absent again from this world
    and alive, again, in another,
        for thirty years
           sleepy and amazed,

rising out of the rough weeds,
    listening and looking.
        Beautiful girl,
           where are you?

OCTOBER

1.

There's this shape, black as the entrance to a cave.
A longing wells up in its throat
like a blossom
as it breathes slowly.

What does the world
mean to you if you can't trust it
to go on shining when you're

not there? And there's
a tree, long-fallen; once
the bees flew to it, like a procession
of messengers, and filled it
with honey.

2.

I said to the chickadee, singing his heart out in the
    green pine tree:

little dazzler,
little song,
little mouthful.

3.

The shape climbs up out of the curled grass. It
grunts into view. There is no measure

for the confidence at the bottom of its eyes—
there is no telling
the suppleness of its shoulders as it turns
and yawns.

       Near the fallen tree
something—a leaf snapped loose
from the branch and fluttering down—tries to pull me
into its trap of attention.

4.

It pulls me
into its trap of attention.

And when I turn again, the bear is gone.

5.

Look, hasn't my body already felt
like the body of a flower?

6.

Look, I want to love this world
as though it's the last chance I'm ever going to get
to be alive
and know it.

7.

Sometimes in late summer I won't touch anything, not
the flowers, not the blackberries
brimming in the thickets; I won't drink
from the pond; I won't name the birds or the trees;
I won't whisper my own name.

                                        One morning
the fox came down the hill, glittering and confident,
and didn't see me—and I thought:

so this is the world.
I'm not in it.
It is beautiful.

FROM

House of Light

1990

SOME QUESTIONS YOU MIGHT ASK

Is the soul solid, like iron?
Or is it tender and breakable, like
the wings of a moth in the beak of the owl?
Who has it, and who doesn't?
I keep looking around me.
The face of the moose is as sad
as the face of Jesus.
The swan opens her white wings slowly.
In the fall, the black bear carries leaves into the darkness.
One question leads to another.
Does it have a shape? Like an iceberg?
Like the eye of a hummingbird?
Does it have one lung, like the snake and the scallop?
Why should I have it, and not the anteater
who loves her children?
Why should l have it, and not the camel?
Come to think of it, what about the maple trees?
What about the blue iris?
What about all the little stones, sitting alone in the moonlight?
What about roses, and lemons, and their shining leaves?
What about the grass?

THE BUDDHA'S LAST INSTRUCTION

"Make of yourself a light,"
said the Buddha,
before he died.
I think of this every morning
as the east begins
to tear off its many clouds
of darkness, to send up the first
signal—a white fan
streaked with pink and violet,
even green.
An old man, he lay down
between two sala trees,
and he might have said anything,
knowing it was his final hour.
The light burns upward,
it thickens and settles over the fields.
Around him, the villagers gathered
and stretched forward to listen.
Even before the sun itself
hangs, disattached, in the blue air,
I am touched everywhere
by its ocean of yellow waves.
No doubt he thought of everything
that had happened in his difficult life.
And then I feel the sun itself
as it blazes over the hills,
like a million flowers on fire—
clearly I'm not needed,

yet I feel myself turning
into something of inexplicable value.
Slowly, beneath the branches,
he raised his head.
He looked into the faces of that frightened crowd.

THE SUMMER DAY

Who made the world?
Who made the swan, and the black bear?
Who made the grasshopper?
This grasshopper, I mean—
the one who has flung herself out of the grass,
the one who is eating sugar out of my hand,
who is moving her jaws back and forth instead of up and down—
who is gazing around with her enormous and complicated eyes.
Now she lifts her pale forearms and thoroughly washes her face.
Now she snaps her wings open, and floats away.
I don't know exactly what a prayer is.
I do know how to pay attention, how to fall down
into the grass, how to kneel down in the grass,
how to be idle and blessed, how to stroll through the fields,
which is what I have been doing all day.
Tell me, what else should I have done?
Doesn't everything die at last, and too soon?
Tell me, what is it you plan to do
with your one wild and precious life?

SPRING

Somewhere
   a black bear
      has just risen from sleep
        and is staring

down the mountain.
   All night
      in the brisk and shallow restlessness
        of early spring

I think of her,
   her four black fists
      flicking the gravel,
        her tongue

like a red fire
   touching the grass,
      the cold water.
        There is only one question;

how to love this world.
   I think of her
      rising
        like a black and leafy ledge

to sharpen her claws against
   the silence
      of the trees.
        Whatever else

. . .

my life is
   with its poems
      and its music
         and its glass cities,

it is also this dazzling darkness
   coming
      down the mountain,
         breathing and tasting;

all day I think of her—
   her white teeth,
      her wordlessness,
         her perfect love.

LITTLE OWL WHO LIVES IN THE ORCHARD

His beak could open a bottle,
and his eyes—when he lifts their soft lids—
go on reading something
just beyond your shoulder—
Blake, maybe,
or the Book of Revelation.

Never mind that he eats only
the black-smocked crickets,
and dragonflies if they happen
to be out late over the ponds, and of course
the occasional festal mouse.
Never mind that he is only a memo
from the offices of fear—

it's not size but surge that tells us
when we're in touch with something real,
and when I hear him in the orchard
fluttering
down the little aluminum
ladder of his scream—
when I see his wings open, like two black ferns,

a flurry of palpitations
as cold as sleet
rackets across the marshlands
of my heart,
like a wild spring day.

Somewhere in the universe,
in the gallery of important things,
the babyish owl, ruffled and rakish,
sits on its pedestal.
Dear, dark dapple of plush!
A message, reads the label,
from that mysterious conglomerate:
Oblivion and Co.
The hooked head stares
from its blouse of dark, feathery lace.
It could be a valentine.

THE KOOKABURRAS

In every heart there is a coward and a procrastinator.
In every heart there is a god of flowers, just waiting
to come out of its cloud and lift its wings.
The kookaburras, kingfishers, pressed against the edge of
their cage, they asked me to open the door.
Years later I wake in the night and remember how I said to them,
no, and walked away.
They had the brown eyes of soft-hearted dogs.
They didn't want to do anything so extraordinary, only to fly
home to their river.
By now I suppose the great darkness has covered them.
As for myself, I am not yet a god of even the palest flowers.
Nothing else has changed either.
Someone tosses their white bones to the dung-heap.
The sun shines on the latch of their cage.
I lie in the dark, my heart pounding.

ROSES, LATE SUMMER

What happens
to the leaves after
they turn red and golden and fall
away? What happens

to the singing birds
when they can't sing
any longer? What happens
to their quick wings?

Do you think there is any
personal heaven
for any of us?
Do you think anyone,

the other side of that darkness,
will call to us, meaning us?
Beyond the trees
the foxes keep teaching their children

to live in the valley.
so they never seem to vanish, they are always there
in the blossom of light
that stands up every morning

in the dark sky.
And over one more set of hills,
along the sea,
the last roses have opened their factories of sweetness

. . .

and are giving it back to the world.
If I had another life
I would want to spend it all on some
unstinting happiness.

I would be a fox, or a tree
full of waving branches.
I wouldn't mind being a rose
in a field full of roses.

Fear has not yet occurred to them, nor ambition.
Reason they have not yet thought of.
Neither do they ask how long they must be roses, and then what.
Or any other foolish question.

WHITE OWL FLIES INTO AND
OUT OF THE FIELD

Coming down
out of the freezing sky
with its depths of light,
like an angel,
or a buddha with wings,
it was beautiful
and accurate,
striking the snow and whatever was there
with a force that left the imprint
of the tips of its wings—
five feet apart—and the grabbing
thrust of its feet,
and the indentation of what had been running
through the white valleys
of the snow—

and then it rose, gracefully,
and flew back to the frozen marshes,
to lurk there,
like a little lighthouse,
in the blue shadows—
so I thought:
maybe death
isn't darkness, after all,
but so much light
wrapping itself around us—

as soft as feathers—
that we are instantly weary
of looking, and looking, and shut our eyes,

not without amazement,
and let ourselves be carried,
as through the translucence of mica,
to the river
that is without the least dapple or shadow—
that is nothing but light—scalding, aortal light—
in which we are washed and washed
out of our bones.

SINGAPORE

In Singapore, in the airport,
a darkness was ripped from my eyes.
In the women's restroom, one compartment stood open.
A woman knelt there, washing something
    in the white bowl.

Disgust argued in my stomach
and I felt, in my pocket, for my ticket.

A poem should always have birds in it.
Kingfishers, say, with their bold eyes and gaudy wings,
Rivers are pleasant, and of course trees.
A waterfall, or if that's not possible, a fountain
    rising and falling.
A person wants to stand in a happy place, in a poem.

When the woman turned I could not answer her face.
Her beauty and her embarrassment struggled together, and
    neither could win.
She smiled and I smiled. What kind of nonsense is this?
Everybody needs a job.

Yes, a person wants to stand in a happy place, in a poem.
But first we must watch her as she stares down at her labor,
    which is dull enough.
She is washing the tops of the airport ashtrays, as big as
    hubcaps, with a blue rag.
Her small hands turn the metal, scrubbing and rinsing.
She does not work slowly, nor quickly, but like a river.
Her dark hair is like the wing of a bird.

. . .

I don't doubt for a moment that she loves her life.
And I want her to rise up from the crust and the slop
    and fly down to the river.
This probably won't happen.
But maybe it will.
If the world were only pain and logic, who would want it?

Of course, it isn't.
Neither do I mean anything miraculous, but only
the light that can shine out of a life. I mean
the way she unfolded and refolded the blue cloth,
the way her smile was only for my sake; I mean
the way this poem is filled with trees, and birds.

THE HERMIT CRAB

Once I looked inside
   the darkness
      of a shell folded like a pastry,
         and there was a fancy face—

or almost a face—
   it turned away
      and frisked up its brawny forearms
         so quickly

against the light
   and my looking in
      I scarcely had time to see it,
         gleaming

under the pure white roof
   of old calcium.
      When I set it down, it hurried
         along the tideline

of the sea,
   which was slashing along as usual,
      shouting and hissing
         toward the future,

turning its back
   with every tide on the past,
      leaving the shore littered
         every morning

. . .

with more ornaments of death—
    what a pearly rubble
        from which to choose a house
            like a white flower—

and what a rebellion
    to leap into it
        and hold on,
            connecting everything,
                ·

the past to the future—
    which is of course the miracle—
        which is the only argument there is
            against the sea.

THE KINGFISHER

The kingfisher rises out of the black wave
like a blue flower, in his beak
he carries a silver leaf. I think this is
the prettiest world—so long as you don't mind
a little dying, how could there be a day in your whole life
that doesn't have its splash of happiness?
There are more fish than there are leaves
on a thousand trees, and anyway the kingfisher
wasn't born to think about it, or anything else.
When the wave snaps shut over his blue head, the water
remains water—hunger is the only story
he has ever heard in his life that he could believe.
I don't say he's right. Neither
do I say he's wrong. Religiously he swallows the silver leaf
with its broken red river, and with a rough and easy cry
I couldn't rouse out of my thoughtful body
if my life depended on it, he swings back
over the bright sea to do the same thing, to do it
(as I long to do something, anything) perfectly.

THE SWAN

Across the wide waters
   something comes
      floating—a slim
      and delicate

ship, filled
   with white flowers—
      and it moves
         on its miraculous muscles

as though time didn't exist,
   as though bringing such gifts
      to the dry shore
         was a happiness

almost beyond bearing.
   And now it turns its dark eyes,
      it rearranges
         the clouds of its wings,

it trails
   an elaborate webbed foot,
      the color of charcoal.
         Soon it will be here.

Oh, what shall I do
   when that poppy-colored beak
      rests in my hand?
         Said Mrs. Blake of the poet:

I miss my husband's company—
    he is so often
        in paradise.
            Of course! the path to heaven

doesn't lie down in flat miles.
    It's in the imagination
        with which you perceive
            this world,

and the gestures
    with which you honor it.
        Oh, what will I do, what will I say, when those
            white wings
            touch the shore?

TURTLE

Now I see it—
it nudges with its bulldog head
the slippery stems of the lilies, making them tremble;
and now it noses along in the wake of the little brown teal

who is leading her soft children
from one side of the pond to the other; she keeps
close to the edge
and they follow closely, the good children—

the tender children,
the sweet children, dangling their pretty feet
into the darkness.
And now will come—I can count on it—the murky splash,

the certain victory
of that pink and gassy mouth, and the frantic
circling of the hen while the rest of the chicks
flare away over the water and into the reeds, and my heart

will be most mournful
on their account. But, listen,
what's important?
Nothing's important

except that the great and cruel mystery of the world,
of which this is a part,
not be denied. Once,
I happened to see, on a city street, in summer,

. . .

a dusty, fouled turtle plodding along—
a snapper—
broken out I suppose from some backyard cage—
and I knew what I had to do—

I looked it right in the eyes, and I caught it—
I put it, like a small mountain range,
into a knapsack, and I took it out
of the city, and I let it

down into the dark pond, into
the cool water,
and the light of the lilies,
to live.

THE LOON ON OAK-HEAD POND

cries for three days, in the gray mist.
cries for the north it hopes it can find.

plunges, and comes up with a slapping pickerel.
blinks its red eye.

cries again.

you come every afternoon, and wait to hear it.
you sit a long time, quiet, under the thick pines,
in the silence that follows.

as though it were your own twilight.
as though it were your own vanishing song.

FIVE A.M. IN THE PINEWOODS

I'd seen
their hoofprints in the deep
needles and knew
they ended the long night

under the pines, walking
like two mute
and beautiful women toward
the deeper woods, so I

got up in the dark and
went there. They came
slowly down the hill
and looked at me sitting under

the blue trees, shyly
they stepped
closer and stared
from under their thick lashes and even

nibbled some damp
tassels of weeds. This
is not a poem about a dream,
though it could be.

This is a poem about the world
that is ours, or could be.
Finally
one of them—I swear it!—

. . .

would have come to my arms.
But the other
stamped sharp hoof in the
pine needles like

the tap of sanity,
and they went off together through
the trees. When I woke
I was alone,

I was thinking:
so this is how you swim inward,
so this is how you flow outward,
so this is how you pray.

SOME HERONS

A blue preacher
flew toward the swamp,
in slow motion.

On the leafy banks,
an old Chinese poet,
hunched in the white gown of his wings,

was waiting.
The water
was the kind of dark silk

that has silver lines
shot through it
when it is touched by the wind

or is splashed upward,
in a small, quick flower,
by the life beneath it.

The preacher
made his difficult landing,
his skirts up around his knees.

The poet's eyes
flared, just as a poet's eyes
are said to do

when the poet is awakened
from the forest of meditation.
It was summer.

. . .

It was only a few moments past the sun's rising,
which meant that the whole long sweet day
lay before them.

They greeted each other,
rumpling their gowns for an instant,
and then smoothing them.

They entered the water,
and instantly two more herons—
equally as beautiful—

joined them and stood just beneath them
in the black, polished water
where they fished, all day.

FROM

Dream Work

1986

ONE OR TWO THINGS

1.

Don't bother me.
I've just
been born.

2.

The butterfly's loping flight
carries it through the country of the leaves
delicately, and well enough to get it
where it wants to go, wherever that is, stopping
here and there to fuzzle the damp throats
of flowers and the black mud; up
and down it swings, frenzied and aimless; and sometimes

for long delicious moments it is perfectly
lazy, riding motionless in the breeze on the soft stalk
of some ordinary flower.

3.

The god of dirt
came up to me many times and said
so many wise and delectable things, I lay
on the grass listening
to his dog voice,
crow voice,
frog voice; *now,*
he said, and *now,*
and never once mentioned *forever,*

4.

which has nevertheless always been,
like a sharp iron hoof,
at the center of my mind.

5.

One or two things are all you need
to travel over the blue pond, over the deep
roughage of the trees and through the stiff
flowers of lightning—some deep
memory of pleasure, some cutting
knowledge of pain.

6.

But to lift the hoof!
For that you need
an idea.

7.

For years and years I struggled
just to love my life. And then

the butterfly
rose, weightless, in the wind.
"Don't love your life
too much," it said,

and vanished
into the world.

MORNING POEM

Every morning
the world
is created.
Under the orange

sticks of the sun
the heaped
ashes of the night
turn into leaves again

and fasten themselves to the high branches
and the ponds appear
like black cloth
on which are painted islands

of summer lilies.
If it is your nature
to be happy
you will swim away along the soft trails

for hours, your imagination
alighting everywhere.
And if your spirit
carries within it

the thorn
that is heavier than lead—
if it's all you can do
to keep on trudging—

. . .

there is still
somewhere deep within you
a beast shouting that the earth
is exactly what it wanted—

each pond with its blazing lilies
is a prayer heard and answered
lavishly,
every morning,

whether or not
you have ever dared to be happy,
whether or not
you have ever dared to pray.

WILD GEESE

You do not have to be good.
You do not have to walk on your knees
for a hundred miles through the desert repenting.
You only have to let the soft animal of your body
     love what it loves.
Tell me about despair, yours, and I will tell you mine.
Meanwhile the world goes on.
Meanwhile the sun and the clear pebbles of the rain
are moving across the landscapes,
over the prairies and the deep trees,
the mountains and the rivers.
Meanwhile the wild geese, high in the clean blue air,
are heading home again.
Whoever you are, no matter how lonely,
the world offers itself to your imagination,
calls to you like the wild geese, harsh and exciting—
over and over announcing your place
in the family of things.

SHADOWS

Everyone knows the great energies running amok cast
terrible shadows, that each of the so-called
senseless acts has its thread looping
back through the world and into a human heart.
    And meanwhile
the gold-trimmed thunder
wanders the sky; the river
may be filling the cellars of the sleeping town.
Cyclone, fire, and their merry cousins
    bring us to grief—but these are the hours
with the old wooden-god faces;
we lift them to our shoulders like so many
black coffins, we continue walking
into the future. I don't mean
    there are no bodies in the river,
or bones broken by the wind. I mean
everyone who has heard the lethal train-roar
of the tornado swears there was no mention ever
of any person, or reason—I mean
    the waters rise without any plot upon
history, or even geography. Whatever
power of the earth rampages, we turn to it
dazed but anonymous eyes; whatever
the name of the catastrophe, it is never
    the opposite of love.

THE JOURNEY

One day you finally knew
what you had to do, and began,
though the voices around you
kept shouting
their bad advice—
though the whole house
began to tremble
and you felt the old tug
at your ankles.
"Mend my life!"
each voice cried.
But you didn't stop.
You knew what you had to do,
though the wind pried
with its stiff fingers
at the very foundations—
though their melancholy
was terrible.
It was already late
enough, and a wild night,
and the road full of fallen
branches and stones.
But little by little,
as you left their voices behind,
the stars began to burn
through the sheets of clouds,
and there was a new voice,
which you slowly
recognized as your own,

that kept you company
as you strode deeper and deeper
into the world,
determined to do
the only thing you could do—
determined to save
the only life you could save.

POEM

The spirit
   likes to dress up like this:
      ten fingers,
        ten toes,

shoulders, and all the rest
   at night
      in the black branches,
        in the morning

in the blue branches
   of the world.
      It could float, of course,
        but would rather

plumb rough matter.
   Airy and shapeless thing,
      it needs
        the metaphor of the body,

lime and appetite,
   the oceanic fluids;
      it needs the body's world,
        instinct

and imagination
   and the dark hug of time,
      sweetness
        and tangibility,

. . .

to be understood,
    to be more than pure light
        that burns
            where no one is—

so it enters us—
    in the morning
        shines from brute comfort
            like a stitch of lightning;

and at night
    lights up the deep and wondrous
        drownings of the body
            like a star.

TWO KINDS OF DELIVERANCE

1.

Last night the geese came back,
slanting fast
from the blossom of the rising moon down
to the black pond. A muskrat
swimming in the twilight saw them and hurried

to the secret lodges to tell everyone
spring had come.

And so it had.
By morning when I went out
the last of the ice had disappeared, blackbirds
sang on the shores. Every year
the geese, returning,
do this, I don't
know how.

2.

The curtains opened and there was
an old man in a headdress of feathers,
leather leggings and a vest made
from the skin of some animal. He danced

in a kind of surly rapture, and the trees
in the fields far away
began to mutter and suck up their long roots.
Slowly they advanced until they stood
pressed to the schoolhouse windows.

3.

I don't know
lots of things but I know this: next year
when spring
flows over the starting point I'll think I'm going to
drown in the shimmering miles of it and then
one or two birds will fly me over
the threshold.
                As for the pain
of others, of course it tries to be
abstract, but then

there flares up out of a vanished wilderness, like fire,
still blistering: the wrinkled face
of an old Chippewa
smiling, hating us,
dancing for his life.

BLACK SNAKES

Suddenly
there I was
on the warm rocks—fear
like a mallet
slung against
metal—it was
that sudden,
that loud,
though in truth
there was no sound, only
the rough wing of fright
rushing
through our bodies.
One flowed
under the leaves, the other flared
half its length
into the air
against my body, then swirled
away. Once I had steadied,
I thought: how valiant!
and I wished
I had come softly, I wished
they were my dark friends.
For a moment I stared
through the impossible gates.
Then I saw them, under the vines,
coiled, cringing,
wishing me gone
with their stone eyes.

Not knowing what I would do
next, their tongues
shook like fire
at the echoes of my body—
that column of death
plunging
through the delicate woods.

1945-1985: POEM FOR THE ANNIVERSARY

Sometimes,
walking for hours through the woods,
I don't know what I'm looking for,
maybe for something
shy and beautiful to come
frisking out of the undergrowth.

Once a fawn did just that.
My dog didn't know
what dogs usually do.
And the fawn didn't know.

As for the doe, she was probably
down in Round Pond, swizzling up
the sweet marsh grass and dreaming
that everything was fine.

———◆———

The way I'd like to go on living in this world
wouldn't hurt anything, I'd just go on
walking uphill and downhill, looking around,
and so what if half the time I don't know
what for—

so what if it doesn't come
to a hill of beans—

so what if I vote liberal,

.   .   .

and am Jewish,
or Lutheran—

or a game warden—

or a bingo addict—

and smoke a pipe?

—◦◦◦◦—

In the films of Dachau and Auschwitz and Bergen-Belsen
the dead rise from the earth
and are piled in front of us, the starved
stare across forty years,
and lush, green, musical Germany
shows again its iron claw, which won't

ever be forgotten, which won't
ever be understood, but which did,
slowly, for years, scrape across Europe

—◦◦◦◦—

while the rest of the world
did nothing.

—◦◦◦◦—

Oh, you never saw
such a good leafy place, and
everything was fine, my dog and the fawn
did a little dance,
they didn't get serious.
Then the fawn clambered away through the leaves

.   .   .

and my gentle dog followed me away.

———∞———

Oh, you never saw such a garden!
A hundred kinds of flowers in bloom!
A waterfall, for pleasure and nothing else!
The garden furniture is white,
tables and chairs in the cool shade.
A man sits there, the long afternoon before him.
He is finishing lunch, some kind
of fruit, chicken, and a salad.
A bottle of wine with a thin and beaded neck.

He fills a glass.
You can tell it is real crystal.
He lifts it to his mouth and drinks peacefully.

It is the face of Mengele.

———∞———

Later
the doe came wandering back in the twilight.
She stepped through the leaves. She hesitated,
sniffing the air.

Then she knew everything.

———∞———

The forest grew dark.

She nuzzled her child wildly.

THE SUNFLOWERS

Come with me
   into the field of sunflowers.
      Their faces are burnished disks,
         their dry spines

creak like ship masts,
   their green leaves,
      so heavy and many,
         fill all day with the sticky

sugars of the sun.
   Come with me
      to visit the sunflowers,
         they are shy

but want to be friends;
   they have wonderful stories
      of when they were young—
         the important weather,

the wandering crows.
   Don't be afraid
      to ask them questions!
         Their bright faces,

which follow the sun,
   will listen, and all
      those rows of seeds—
         each one a new life!—

. . .

hope for a deeper acquaintance;
    each of them, though it stands
        in a crowd of many,
           like a separate universe,

is lonely, the long work
    of turning their lives
        into a celebration
           is not easy. Come

and let us talk with those modest faces,
    the simple garments of leaves,
        the coarse roots in the earth
           so uprightly burning.

FROM

American
Primitive

1983

AUGUST

When the blackberries hang
swollen in the woods, in the brambles
nobody owns, I spend

all day among the high
branches, reaching
my ripped arms, thinking

of nothing, cramming
the black honey of summer
into my mouth; all day my body

accepts what it is. In the dark
creeks that run by there is
this thick paw of my life darting among

the black bells, the leaves; there is
this happy tongue.

THE KITTEN

More amazed than anything
I took the perfectly black
stillborn kitten
with the one large eye
in the center of its small forehead
from the house cat's bed
and buried it in a field
behind the house.

I suppose I could have given it
to a museum,
I could have called the local
newspaper.

But instead I took it out into the field
and opened the earth
and put it back
saying, it was real,
saying, life is infinitely inventive,
saying, what other amazements
lie in the dark seed of the earth, yes,

I think I did right to go out alone
and give it back peacefully, and cover the place
with the reckless blossoms of weeds.

MOLES

Under the leaves, under
the first loose
levels of earth
they're there—quick
as beetles, blind
as bats, shy
as hares but seen
less than these—
traveling
among the pale girders
of appleroot,
rockshelf, nests
of insects and black
pastures of bulbs
peppery and packed full
of the sweetest food:
spring flowers.
Field after field
you can see the traceries
of their long
lonely walks, then
the rains blur
even this frail
hint of them—
so excitable,
so plush,
so willing to continue
generation after generation
accomplishing nothing

but their brief physical lives
as they live and die,
pushing and shoving
with their stubborn muzzles against
the whole earth,
finding it
delicious.

CLAPP'S POND

Three miles through the woods
Clapp's Pond sprawls stone gray
among oaks and pines,
the late winter fields

where a pheasant blazes up
lifting his yellow legs
under bronze feathers, opening
bronze wings;

and one doe, dimpling the ground as she touches
its dampness sharply, flares
out of the brush and gallops away.

By evening: rain.
It pours down from the black clouds,
lashes over the roof. The last
acorns spray over the porch; I toss
one, then two more
logs on the fire.

How sometimes everything
closes up, a painted fan, landscapes and moments
flowing together until the sense of distance—
say, between Clapp's Pond and me—
vanishes, edges slide together

like the feathers of a wing, everything
touches everything.

Later, lying half-asleep under
the blankets, I watch
while the doe, glittering with rain, steps
under the wet slabs of the pines, stretches
her long neck down to drink

---

from the pond
three miles away.

FIRST SNOW

The snow
began here
this morning and all day
continued, its white
rhetoric everywhere
calling us back to *why, how,*
whence such beauty and *what*
the meaning; such
an oracular fever! flowing
past windows, an energy it seemed
would never ebb, never settle
less than lovely! and only now,
deep into night,
it has finally ended.
The silence
is immense,
and the heavens still hold
a million candles; nowhere
the familiar things:
stars, the moon,
the darkness we expect
and nightly turn from. Trees
glitter like castles
of ribbons, the broad fields
smolder with light, a passing
creekbed lies
heaped with shining hills;
and though the questions
that have assailed us all day

remain—not a single
answer has been found—
walking out now
into the silence and the light
under the trees,
and through the fields,
feels like one.

GHOSTS

1.

Have you noticed?

2.

Where so many millions of powerful bawling beasts
lay down on the earth and died
it's hard to tell now
what's bone, and what merely
was once.

The golden eagle, for instance,
has a bit of heaviness in him;
moreover the huge barns
seem ready, sometimes, to ramble off
toward deeper grass.

3.

1805
near the Bitterroot Mountains:
a man named Lewis kneels down
on the prairie watching

a sparrow's nest cleverly concealed in the wild hyssop
and lined with buffalo hair. The chicks,
not more than a day hatched, lean
quietly into the thick wool as if
content, after all,
to have left the perfect world and fallen,

. . .

helpless and blind
into the flowered fields and the perils
of this one.

4.

In the book of the earth it is written:
nothing can die.

In the book of the Sioux it is written:
they have gone away into the earth to hide.
Nothing will coax them out again
but the people dancing.

5.

Said the old-timers:
the tongue
is the sweetest meat.

Passengers shooting from train windows
could hardly miss, they were
that many.

Afterward the carcasses
stank unbelievably, and sang with flies, ribboned
with slopes of white fat,
black ropes of blood—hellhunks
in the prairie heat.

6.

Have you noticed? how the rain
falls soft as the fall
of moccasins. *Have you noticed?*
how the immense circles still,
stubbornly, after a hundred years,
mark the grass where the rich droppings
from the roaring bulls
fell to the earth as the herd stood
day after day, moon after moon
in their tribal circle, outwaiting
the packs of yellow-eyed wolves that are also
have you noticed? gone now.

7.

Once only, and then in a dream,
I watched while, secretly
and with the tenderness of any caring woman,
a cow gave birth
to a red calf, tongued him dry and nursed him
in a warm corner
of the clear night
in the fragrant grass
in the wild domains
of the prairie spring, and I asked them,
in my dream I knelt down and asked them
to make room for me.

SKUNK CABBAGE

And now as the iron rinds over
the ponds start dissolving,
you come, dreaming of ferns and flowers
and new leaves unfolding,
upon the brash
turnip-hearted skunk cabbage
slinging its bunched leaves up
through the chilly mud.
You kneel beside it. The smell
is lurid and flows out in the most
unabashed way, attracting
into itself a continual spattering
of protein. Appalling its rough
green caves, and the thought
of the thick root nested below, stubborn
and powerful as instinct!
But these are the woods you love,
where the secret name
of every death is life again—a miracle
wrought surely not of mere turning
but of dense and scalding reenactment. Not
tenderness, not longing, but daring and brawn
pull down the frozen waterfall, the past.
Ferns, leaves, flowers, the last subtle
refinements, elegant and easeful, wait
to rise and flourish.
What blazes the trail is not necessarily pretty.

THE SNAKES

I once saw two snakes,
northern racers,
hurrying through the woods,
their bodies
like two black whips
lifting and dashing forward;
in perfect concert
they held their heads high
and swam forward
on their sleek bellies;
under the trees,
through vines, branches,
over stones,
through fields of flowers,
they traveled
like a matched team
like a dance
like a love affair.

WHITE NIGHT

All night
  I float
    in the shallow ponds
      while the moon wanders
burning,
  bone white,
    among the milky stems.
    Once
I saw her hand reach
  to touch the muskrat's
    small sleek head
      and it was lovely, oh,
I don't want to argue anymore
  about all the things
    I thought I could not
      live without! Soon
the muskrat
  will glide with another
    into their castle
      of weeds, morning
will rise from the east
  tangled and brazen,
    and before that
    difficult
and beautiful
  hurricane of light
    I want to flow out
      across the mother

of all waters,
   I want to lose myself
      on the black
         and silky currents,
yawning,
   gathering
      the tall lilies
         of sleep.

THE FISH

The first fish
I ever caught
would not lie down
quiet in the pail
but flailed and sucked
at the burning
amazement of the air
and died
in the slow pouring off
of rainbows. Later
I opened his body and separated
the flesh from the bones
and ate him. Now the sea
is in me: I am the fish, the fish
glitters in me; we are
risen, tangled together, certain to fall
back to the sea. Out of pain,
and pain, and more pain
we feed this feverish plot, we are nourished
by the mystery.

HUMPBACKS

There is, all around us,
this country
of original fire.

You know what I mean.

The sky, after all, stops at nothing, so something
    has to be holding
our bodies
in its rich and timeless stables or else
we would fly away.

Off Stellwagen
off the Cape,
the humpbacks rise. Carrying their tonnage
    of barnacles and joy
they leap through the water, they nuzzle back under it
like children
at play.

They sing, too.
And not for any reason
you can't imagine.

Three of them
rise to the surface near the bow of the boat,
then dive
deeply, their huge scarred flukes
tipped to the air.

We wait, not knowing
just where it will happen; suddenly
they smash through the surface, someone begins
shouting for joy and you realize
it is yourself as they surge
upward and you see for the first time
how huge they are, as they breach,
and dive, and breach again
through the shining blue flowers
of the split water and you see them
for some unbelievable
part of a moment against the sky—
like nothing you've ever imagined—
like the myth of the fifth morning galloping
out of darkness, pouring
heavenward, spinning; then

---

they crash back under those black silks
and we all fall back
together into that wet fire, you
know what I mean.

I know a captain who has seen them
playing with seaweed, swimming
through the green islands, tossing
the slippery branches into the air.

I know a whale that will come to the boat whenever
she can, and nudge it gently along the bow
with her long flipper.

I know several lives worth living.

———∞———

Listen, whatever it is you try
to do with your life, nothing will ever dazzle you
like the dreams of your body,

its spirit
longing to fly while the dead-weight bones

toss their dark mane and hurry
back into the fields of glittering fire

where everything,
even the great whale,
throbs with song.

A MEETING

She steps into the dark swamp
where the long wait ends.

The secret slippery package
drops to the weeds.

She leans her long neck and tongues it
between breaths slack with exhaustion

and after a while it rises and becomes a creature
like her, but much smaller.

So now there are two. And they walk together
like a dream under the trees.

In early June, at the edge of a field
thick with pink and yellow flowers

I meet them.
I can only stare.

She is the most beautiful woman
I have ever seen.

Her child leaps among the flowers,
the blue of the sky falls over me

like silk, the flowers burn, and I want
to live my life all over again, to begin again,

to be utterly
wild.

THE ROSES

One day in summer
when everything
has already been more than enough
the wild beds start
exploding open along the berm
of the sea; day after day
you sit near them; day after day
the honey keeps on coming
in the red cups and the bees
like amber drops roll
in the petals: there is no end,
believe me! to the inventions of summer,
to the happiness your body
is willing to bear.

BLACKBERRIES

I come down.
Come down the blacktop road from Red Rock.
A hot day.

Off the road in the hacked tangles
blackberries big as thumbs hang shining
in the shade. And a creek nearby: a dark
spit through wet stones. And a pool

like a stonesink if you know
where to climb for it among
the hillside ferns, where the thrush
naps in her nest of sticks and loam. I

come down from Red Rock, lips streaked
black, fingers purple, throat cool, shirt
full of fernfingers, head full of windy
whistling. It

takes all day.

TECUMSEH

I went down not long ago
to the Mad River, under the willows
I knelt and drank from that crumpled flow, call it
what madness you will, there's a sickness
worse than the risk of death and that's
forgetting what we should never forget.
Tecumseh lived here.
The wounds of the past
are ignored, but hang on
like the litter that snags among the yellow branches,
newspapers and plastic bags, after the rains.

Where are the Shawnee now?
Do you know? Or would you have to
write to Washington, and even then,
whatever they said,
would you believe it? Sometimes

I would like to paint my body red and go out into
the glittering snow
to die.

His name meant Shooting Star.
From Mad River country north to the border
he gathered the tribes
and armed them one more time. He vowed
to keep Ohio and it took him
over twenty years to fail.

After the bloody and final fighting, at Thames,
it was over, except
his body could not be found.
It was never found,
and you can do whatever you want with that, say

his people came in the black leaves of the night
and hauled him to a secret grave, or that
he turned into a little boy again, and leaped
into a birch canoe and went
rowing home down the rivers. Anyway,
this much I'm sure of: if we ever meet him, we'll know it,
he will still be
so angry.

IN BLACKWATER WOODS

Look, the trees
are turning
their own bodies
into pillars

of light,
are giving off the rich
fragrance of cinnamon
and fulfillment,

the long tapers
of cattails
are bursting and floating away over
the blue shoulders

of the ponds,
and every pond,
no matter what its
name is, is

nameless now.
Every year
everything
I have ever learned

in my lifetime
leads back to this: the fires
and the black river of loss
whose other side

. . .

is salvation,
whose meaning
none of us will ever know.
To live in this world

you must be able
to do three things:
to love what is mortal;
to hold it

against your bones knowing
your own life depends on it;
and, when the time comes to let it go,
to let it go.

FROM

Three Rivers
Poetry Journal

1980

and "Three Poems
for James Wright"

1982

AT BLACKWATER POND

At Blackwater Pond the tossed waters have settled
after a night of rain.
I dip my cupped hands. I drink
a long time. It tastes
like stone, leaves, fire. It falls cold
into my body, waking the bones. I hear them
deep inside me, whispering
oh what is that beautiful thing
that just happened?

THE RABBIT

Scatterghost,
it can't float away.
And the rain, everybody's brother,
won't help. And the wind all these days
flying like ten crazy sisters everywhere
can't seem to do a thing. No one but me,
and my hands like fire,
to lift him to a last burrow. I wait

days, while the body opens and begins
to boil. I remember

the leaping in the moonlight, and can't touch it,
wanting it miraculously to heal
and spring up
joyful. But finally

I do. And the day after I've shoveled
the earth over, in a field nearby

I find a small bird's nest lined pale
and silvery and the chicks—

are you listening, death?—warm in the rabbit's fur.

THREE POEMS FOR JAMES WRIGHT

1. Hearing of Your Illness

I went out
from the news of your illness
like a broken bone

I spoke your name
to the sickle moon and saw her white wing
fall back toward the blackness, but she
rowed deep past that hesitation, and
kept rising.

Then I went down
to a black creek and alder grove
that is Ohio like nothing else is
and told them. There was an owl there,
sick of its hunger but still
trapped in it, unable to be anything else.
And the creek
tippled on down over some dark rocks
and the alders
breathed fast in their red blossoms.

Then I lay down in a rank and spring-sweet field.
Weeds sprouting in the darkness, and some
small creatures rustling about, living their lives
as they do, moment by moment.

I felt better, telling them about you.
They know what pain is, and they knew you,

and they would have stopped too, as I
was longing to do, everything, the hunger
and the flowing.

That they could not—
merely loved you and waited
to take you back

as a stone,
as a small quick Ohio creek,
as the beautiful pulse of everything,
meanwhile not missing one shred of their own

assignments of song
and muscle—
was what I learned there, so I

got up finally, with a grief
worthy of you, and went home.

2. Early Morning in Ohio

A late snowfall.
In the white morning the trains
whistle and bang in the freightyard,
shifting track, getting ready
to get on with it, to roll out
into the country again, to get
far away from here and closer
to somewhere else.

. . .

A mile away, leaving the house, I hear them
and stop, astonished.

Of course. I thought they would stop
when you did. I thought you'd never sicken
anyway, or, if you did, Ohio
would fall down too, barn
by bright barn, into

hillsides of pain: torn boards,
bent nails, shattered
windows. My old dog

who doesn't know yet he is only mortal
bounds limping away
through the weeds, and I don't do
anything to stop him.

I remember
what you said.

And think how somewhere in Tuscany
a small spider might even now
be stepping forth, testing
the silks of her web, the morning air,
the possibilities; maybe even, who knows,
singing a tiny song.

And if the whistling of the trains drags through me
like wire, well, I can hurt can't I? The white fields

burn or my eyes swim, whichever; anyway I whistle
to the old dog and when he comes finally

I fall to my knees in the glittering snow, I throw
my arms around him.

3. The Rose

I had a red rose to send you,
but it reeked of occasion, I thought,
so I didn't. Anyway
it was the time
the willows do what they do
every spring, so I cut some
down by a dark Ohio creek and was ready
to mail them to you when the news came
that nothing
could come to you
in time
anymore
ever.

I put down the phone
and I thought I saw, on the floor of the room, suddenly,
a large box,
and I knew, the next thing I had to do,
was lift it
and I didn't know if I could.

. . .

Well, I did.
But don't call it anything
but what it was—the voice
of a small bird singing inside, Lord,
how it sang, and kept singing!
how it keeps singing!

in its deep
and miraculous
composure.

FROM

Twelve Moons

1979

SLEEPING IN THE FOREST

I thought the earth
remembered me, she
took me back so tenderly, arranging
her dark skirts, her pockets
full of lichens and seeds. I slept
as never before, a stone
on the riverbed, nothing
between me and the white fire of the stars
but my thoughts, and they floated
light as moths among the branches
of the perfect trees. All night
I heard the small kingdoms breathing
around me, the insects, and the birds
who do their work in the darkness. All night
I rose and fell, as if in water, grappling
with a luminous doom. By morning
I had vanished at least a dozen times
into something better.

SNAKES IN WINTER

Deep in the woods,
under the sprawled upheavals of rocks,

dozens lie coiled together.
Touch them: they scarcely

breathe; they stare
out of such deep forgetfulness

that their eyes are like jewels—
and asleep, though they cannot close.

And in each mouth the forked tongue,
sensitive as an angel's ear,

lies like a drugged muscle.
With the fires of spring they will lash forth again

on their life of ribs!—
bodies like whips!

But now under the lids of the mute
succeeding snowfalls

they sleep in their cold cauldron: a flickering broth
six months below simmer.

MUSIC LESSONS

Sometimes, in the middle of the lesson,
we exchanged places. She would gaze a moment at her
    hands
spread over the keys; then the small house with its knick-
    knacks,
its shut windows,

its photographs of her sons and the serious husband,
vanished as new shapes formed. Sound
became music, and music a white
scarp for the listener to climb

alone. I leaped rock over rock to the top
and found myself waiting, transformed,
and still she played, her eyes luminous and willful,
her pinned hair falling down—

forgetting me, the house, the neat green yard,
she fled in that lick of flame all tedious bonds:
supper, the duties of flesh and home,
the knife at the throat, the death in the metronome.

ENTERING THE KINGDOM

The crows see me.
They stretch their glossy necks
In the tallest branches
Of green trees. I am
Possibly dangerous, I am
Entering the kingdom.

The dream of my life
Is to lie down by a slow river
And stare at the light in the trees—
To learn something by being nothing
A little while but the rich
Lens of attention.

But the crows puff their feathers and cry
Between me and the sun,
And I should go now.
They know me for what I am.
No dreamer,
No eater of leaves.

THE NIGHT TRAVELER

Passing by, he could be anybody:
A thief, a tradesman, a doctor
On his way to a worried house.
But when he stops at your gate,
Under the room where you lie half-asleep,
You know it is not just anyone—
It is the Night Traveler.

You lean your arms on the sill
And stare down. But all you can see
Are bits of wilderness attached to him—
Twigs, loam and leaves,
Vines and blossoms. Among these
You feel his eyes, and his hands
Lifting something in the air.

He has a gift for you, but it has no name.
It is windy and woolly.
He holds it in the moonlight, and it sings
Like a newborn beast,
Like a child at Christmas,
Like your own heart as it tumbles
In love's green bed.
You take it, and he is gone.

All night—and all your life, if you are willing—
It will nuzzle your face, cold-nosed,
Like a small white wolf;
It will curl in your palm

Like a hard blue stone;
It will liquefy into a cold pool
Which, when you dive into it,
Will hold you like a mossy jaw.
A bath of light. An answer.

BEAVER MOON—THE SUICIDE OF A FRIEND

When somewhere life
breaks like a pane of glass,
and from every direction casual
voices are bringing you the news,
you say: I should have known.
You say: I should have been aware.
That last Friday he looked
so ill, like an old mountain-climber
lost on the white trails, listening
to the ice breaking upward, under
his worn-out shoes. You say:
I heard rumors of trouble, but after all
we all have that. You say:
what could I have done? and you go
with the rest, to bury him.
That night, you turn in your bed
to watch the moon rise, and once more
see what a small coin it is
against the darkness, and how everything else
is a mystery, and you know
nothing at all except
the moonlight is beautiful—
white rivers running together
along the bare boughs of the trees—
and somewhere, for someone, life
is becoming moment by moment
unbearable.

LAST DAYS

Things are
    changing; things are starting to
        spin, snap, fly off into
            the blue sleeve of the long
                afternoon. *Oh* and *ooh*
come whistling out of the perished mouth
    of the grass, as things
turn soft, boil back
    into substance and hue. As everything,
        forgetting its own enchantment, whispers:
           I too love oblivion why not it is full
         of second chances. *Now,*
hiss the bright curls of the leaves. *Now!*
    booms the muscle of the wind.

THE BLACK SNAKE

When the black snake
flashed onto the morning road,
and the truck could not swerve—
death, that is how it happens.

Now he lies looped and useless
as an old bicycle tire.
I stop the car
and carry him into the bushes.

He is as cool and gleaming
as a braided whip, he is as beautiful and quiet
as a dead brother.
I leave him under the leaves

and drive on, thinking
about *death*: its suddenness,
its terrible weight,
its certain coming. Yet under

reason burns a brighter fire, which the bones
have always preferred.
It is the story of endless good fortune.
It says to oblivion: not me!

It is the light at the center of every cell.
It is what sent the snake coiling and flowing forward
happily all spring through the green leaves before
he came to the road.

THE TRURO BEAR

There's a bear in the Truro woods.
People have seen it—three or four,
or two, or one. I think
of the thickness of the serious woods
around the dark bowls of the Truro ponds;
I think of the blueberry fields, the blackberry tangles,
the cranberry bogs. And the sky
with its new moon, its familiar star-trails,
burns down like a brand-new heaven,
while everywhere I look on the scratchy hillsides
shadows seem to grow shoulders. Surely
a beast might be clever, be lucky, move quietly
through the woods for years, learning to stay away
from roads and houses. Common sense mutters:
it can't be true, it must be somebody's
runaway dog. But the seed
has been planted, and when has happiness ever
required much evidence to begin
its leaf-green breathing?

MUSSELS

In the riprap,
   in the cool caves,
      in the dim and salt-refreshed
      recesses, they cling
in dark clusters,
   in barnacled fistfuls,
      in the dampness that never
      leaves, in the deeps
of high tide, in the slow
   washing away of the water
      in which they feed,
      in which the blue shells
open a little, and the orange bodies
   make a sound,
      not loud,
      not unmusical, as they take
nourishment, as the ocean
   enters their bodies. At low tide
      I am on the riprap, clattering
      with boots and a pail,
rock over rock; I choose
   the crevice, I reach
      forward into the dampness,
      my hands feeling everywhere
for the best, the biggest. Even before
   I decide which to take,
      which to twist from the wet rocks,
      which to devour,

they, who have no eyes to see with,
    see me, like a shadow,
        bending forward. Together
            they make a sound,
not loud,
    not unmusical, as they lean
        into the rocks, away
            from my grasping fingers.

SNOW MOON—BLACK BEAR GIVES BIRTH

It was not quite spring, it was
the gray flux before.

Out of the black wave of sleep she turned,
enormous beast,

and welcomed the little ones, blind pink islands
no bigger than shoes. She washed them;

she nibbled them with teeth like white tusks;
   she curled down
beside them like a horizon.

They snuggled. Each knew what it was:
an original, formed

in the whirlwind, with no recognitions between
itself and the first steams

of creation. Together they nuzzled
her huge flank until she spilled over,

and they pummeled and pulled her tough nipples, and she
   gave them
the rich river.

STRAWBERRY MOON

1.

My great-aunt Elizabeth Fortune
stood under the honey locust trees,
the white moon over her and a young man near.
The blossoms fell down like white feathers,
the grass was warm as a bed, and the young man
full of promises, and the face of the moon
a white fire.

Later,
when the young man went away and came back with a
    bride,
Elizabeth
climbed into the attic.

2.

Three women came in the night
to wash the blood away,
and burn the sheets,
and take away the child.

Was it a boy or girl?
No one remembers.

3.

Elizabeth Fortune was not seen again
for forty years

. . .

Meals were sent up,
laundry exchanged.

It was considered a solution
more proper than shame
showing itself to the village.

4.

Finally, name by name, the downstairs died
or moved away,
and she had to come down,
so she did.

At sixty-one, she took in boarders,

washed their dishes,
made their beds,
spoke whatever had to be spoken,
and no more.

5.

I asked my mother:
what happened to the man? She answered:
Nothing.
They had three children.
He worked in the boatyard.

I asked my mother: did they ever meet again?
No, she said,
though sometimes he would come
to the house to visit.
Elizabeth, of course, stayed upstairs.

6.

Now the women are gathering
in smoke-filled rooms,
rough as politicians,
scrappy as club fighters.
And should anyone be surprised

if sometimes, when the white moon rises,
women want to lash out
with a cutting edge?

PINK MOON—THE POND

You think it will never happen again.
Then, one night in April,
the tribes wake trilling.
You walk down to the shore.
Your coming stills them,
but little by little the silence lifts
until song is everywhere
and your soul rises from your bones
and strides out over the water.
It is a crazy thing to do—
for no one can live like that,
floating around in the darkness
over the gauzy water.
Left on the shore your bones
keep shouting *come back!*
But your soul won't listen;
in the distance it is unfolding
like a pair of wings, it is sparking
like hot wires. So,
like a good friend,
you decide to follow.
You step off the shore
and plummet to your knees—
you slog forward to your thighs
and sink to your cheekbones—
and now you are caught
by the cold chains of the water—
you are vanishing while around you
the frogs continue to sing, driving

their music upward through your own throat,
not even noticing
you are something else.
And that's when it happens—
you see everything
through their eyes,
their joy, their necessity;
you wear their webbed fingers;
your throat swells.
And that's when you know
you will live whether you will or not,
one way or another,
because everything is everything else,
one long muscle.
It's no more mysterious than that.
So you relax, you don't fight it anymore,
the darkness coming down
called water,
called spring,
called the green leaf, called
a woman's body
as it turns into mud and leaves,
as it beats in its cage of water,
as it turns like a lonely spindle
in the moonlight, as it says
yes.

AUNT LEAF

Needing one, I invented her—
the great-great-aunt dark as hickory
called Shining-Leaf, or Drifting-Cloud
or The-Beauty-of-the-Night.

Dear aunt, I'd call into the leaves,
and she'd rise up, like an old log in a pool,
and whisper in a language only the two of us knew
the word that meant *follow*,

and we'd travel
cheerful as birds
out of the dusty town and into the trees
where she would change us both into something quicker—
two foxes with black feet,
two snakes green as ribbons,
two shimmering fish—
and all day we'd travel.

At day's end she'd leave me back at my own door
with the rest of my family,
who were kind, but solid as wood
and rarely wandered. While she,
old twist of feathers and birch bark,
would walk in circles wide as rain and then
float back

scattering the rags of twilight
on fluttering moth wings;

. . .

or she'd slouch from the barn like a gray opossum;

or she'd hang in the milky moonlight
burning like a medallion,

this bone dream,
this friend I had to have,
this old woman made out of leaves.

FARM COUNTRY

I have sharpened my knives, I have
Put on the heavy apron.

Maybe you think life is chicken soup, served
In blue willow-pattern bowls.

I have put on my boots and opened
The kitchen door and stepped out

Into the sunshine. I have crossed the lawn,
I have entered

The hen house.

THE LAMPS

Eight o'clock, no later,
You light the lamps,

The big one by the large window,
The small one on your desk.

They are not to see by—
It is still twilight out over the sand,

The scrub oaks and cranberries.
Even the small birds have not settled

For sleep yet, out of the reach
Of prowling foxes. No,

You light the lamps because
You are alone in your small house

And the wicks sputtering gold
Are like two visitors with good stories

They will tell slowly, in soft voices,
While the air outside turns quietly

A grainy and luminous blue.
You wish it would never change—

. . .

But of course the darkness keeps
Its appointment. Each evening,

An inscrutable presence, it has the final word
Outside every door.

FROM

The River Styx, Ohio

Ohio

1972

LEARNING ABOUT THE INDIANS

He danced in feathers, with paint across his nose.
Thump, thump went the drum, and bumped our blood,
And sent a strange vibration through the mind.
White Eagle, he was called, or Mr. White,

And he strutted for money now, in schoolrooms built
On Ohio's plains, surrounded by the graves
Of all of our fathers, but more of his than ours.
Our teachers called it Extracurricular.

We called it fun. And as for Mr. White,
Changed back to a shabby salesman's suit, he called it
Nothing at all as he packed his drums, and drove,
Tires screeching, out of the schoolyard into the night.

GOING TO WALDEN

It isn't very far as highways lie.
I might be back by nightfall, having seen
The rough pines, and the stones, and the clear water.
Friends argue that I might be wiser for it.
They do not hear that far-off Yankee whisper:
How dull we grow from hurrying here and there!

Many have gone, and think me half a fool
To miss a day away in the cool country.
Maybe. But in a book I read and cherish,
Going to Walden is not so easy a thing
As a green visit. It is the slow and difficult
Trick of living, and finding it where you are.

NIGHT FLIGHT

Traveling at thirty thousand feet, we see
How much of earth still lies in wilderness,
Till terminals occur like miracles
To civilize the paralyzing dark.

Buckled for landing to a tilting chair,
I think: if miracle or accident
Should send us on across the upper air,
How many miles, or nights, or years to go
Before the mind, with its huge ego paling,
Before the heart, all expectation spent,
Should read the meaning of the scene below?

But now already the loved ones gather
Under the dome of welcome, as we glide
Over the final jutting mountainside,
Across the suburbs tangled in their lights,

And settled softly on the earth once more
Rise in the fierce assumption of our lives—
Discarding smoothly, as we disembark,
All thoughts that held us wiser for a moment
Up there alone, in the impartial dark.

FROM

No Voyage and Other Poems

1963 and 1965

NO VOYAGE

I wake earlier, now that the birds have come
And sing in the unfailing trees.
On a cot by an open window
I lie like land used up, while spring unfolds.

Now of all voyagers I remember, who among them
Did not board ship with grief among their maps?—
Till it seemed men never go somewhere, they only leave
Wherever they are, when the dying begins.

For myself, I find my wanting life
Implores no novelty and no disguise of distance;
Where, in what country, might I put down these thoughts,
Who still am citizen of this fallen city?

On a cot by an open window, I lie and remember
While the birds in the trees sing of the circle of time.
Let the dying go on, and let me, if I can,
Inherit from disaster before I move.

O, I go to see the great ships ride from harbor,
And my wounds leap with impatience; yet I turn back
To sort the weeping ruins of my house:
Here or nowhere I will make peace with the fact.

JACK

The wagons stand
And rust, and glitter sometimes in the moon,
Since we have lost dominion of the fields.
No more great clattering Jack,
His thick mane filled with chaff and wind,
Will let us lead him from the easy barns;
No more sweet gentle Jack
Will let us strap him to his leather bondage
And help us tow the weight of summer home.

The days
Are easier now, and we have time for thought,
Idling in corners of our weedy land.
But now we learn, as season follows season
And no one plants upon these hills,
How poor a gift is freedom to the spirit
That loved the labor. Now, like Jack,
We stand turned out into eternal Sunday,
And look through moonlight at the silenced wagons.

Yet we have lives to balance our regret,
Can turn to other things.
Now in the moonlight we can move away,
While he is left staring upon the stark
Arrangement of the wagons leaning earthward:
The simple blood that cannot name its lack,
But knows the world has fallen out of reason,
That it is autumn, and no laborer comes.

BEYOND THE SNOW BELT

Over the local stations, one by one,
Announcers list disasters like dark poems
That always happen in the skull of winter.
But once again the storm has passed us by:
Lovely and moderate, the snow lies down
While shouting children hurry back to play,
And scarved and smiling citizens once more
Sweep down their easy paths of pride and welcome.

And what else might we do? Let us be truthful.
Two counties north the storm has taken lives.
Two counties north, to us, is far away,—
A land of trees, a wing upon a map,
A wild place never visited,—so we
Forget with ease each far mortality.

Peacefully from our frozen yards we watch
Our children running on the mild white hills.
This is the landscape that we understand,—
And till the principle of things takes root,
How shall examples move us from our calm?
I do not say that it is not a fault.
I only say, except as we have loved,
All news arrives as from a distant land.

THE SWIMMING LESSON

Feeling the icy kick, the endless waves
Reaching around my life, I moved my arms
And coughed, and in the end saw land.

Somebody, I suppose,
Remembering the medieval maxim,
Had tossed me in,
Had wanted me to learn to swim,

Not knowing that none of us, who ever came back
From that long lonely fall and frenzied rising,
Ever learned anything at all
About swimming, but only
How to put off, one by one,
Dreams and pity, love and grace,—
How to survive in any place.

ON WINTER'S MARGIN

On winter's margin, see the small birds now
With half-forged memories come flocking home
To gardens famous for their charity.
The green globe's broken; vines like tangled veins
Hang at the entrance to the silent wood.

With half a loaf, I am the prince of crumbs;
By time snow's down, the birds amassed will sing
Like children for their sire to walk abroad!
But what I love, is the gray stubborn hawk
Who floats alone beyond the frozen vines;
And what I dream of are the patient deer
Who stand on legs like reeds and drink the wind;—

They are what saves the world: who choose to grow
Thin to a starting point beyond this squalor.

THE RETURN

The deed took all my heart.
I did not think of you,
Not till the thing was done.
I put my sword away,
And then no more the cold
And perfect fury ran
Along my narrow bones,
And then no more the black
And dripping corridors
Held anywhere the shape
That I had come to slay.
Then, for the first time,
I saw in the cave's belly
The dark and clotted webs,
The green and sucking pools,
The rank and crumbling walls,
The maze of passages.

And I thought then
Of the far earth,
Of the spring sun
And the slow wind,
And a young girl.
And I looked then
At the white thread.

Hunting the minotaur
I was no common man
And had no need of love.
I trailed the shining thread

Behind me, for a vow,
And did not think of you.
It lay there, like a sign,
Coiled on the bull's great hoof
And back into the world.
Half blind with weariness
I touched the thread and wept.
O, it was frail as air.

And I turned then
With the white spool
Through the cold rocks,
Through the black rocks,
Through the long webs,
And the mist fell,
And the webs clung,
And the rocks tumbled,
And the earth shook.

And the thread held.

MORNING IN A NEW LAND

In trees still dripping night some nameless birds
Woke, shook out their arrowy wings, and sang,
Slowly, like finches sifting through a dream.
The pink sun fell, like glass, into the fields.
Two chestnuts, and a dapple gray,
Their shoulders wet with light, their dark hair streaming,
Climbed the hill. The last mist fell away,

And under the trees, beyond time's brittle drift,
I stood like Adam in his lonely garden
On that first morning, shaken out of sleep,
Rubbing his eyes, listening, parting the leaves,
Like tissue on some vast, incredible gift.

Acknowledgments

Grateful acknowledgment is made for the permission to reprint the following works:

Poems from *Felicity* by Mary Oliver (Penguin Press). Copyright © 2015 by Mary Oliver. Used by permission of Charlotte Sheedy Literary Agency.

Poems from *Blue Horses* by Mary Oliver (Penguin Press). Copyright © 2014 by Mary Oliver. Used by permission of Charlotte Sheedy Literary Agency.

"Benjamin, Who Came From Who Knows Where," "Bazougey," and "The Poetry Teacher" from *Dog Songs* by Mary Oliver (Penguin Press). Copyright © 2013 by Mary Oliver. Used by permission of Charlotte Sheedy Literary Agency.

Devotions is arranged by date of publication, but in the instance of *Dog Songs*, a volume collecting many earlier poems, it was worth a bit of mischief to allow all the dogs to be together. Poems originally published elsewhere: "The Storm" from *Winter Hours*, "Percy (One)" and "Little Dog's Rhapsody in the Night (Percy Three)" from *New and Selected Poems: Volume Two*, "Percy (Nine)" from *Red Bird*, "The Dog Has Run Off Again" from *West Wind*, "Her Grave" from *New and Selected Poems: Volume One*, and "The First Time Percy Came Back" from *A Thousand Mornings*.

Poems from *A Thousand Mornings* by Mary Oliver (Penguin Press). Copyright © 2012 by Mary Oliver. Used by permission of Charlotte Sheedy Literary Agency.

Poems from *Swan* by Mary Oliver. Copyright © 2010 by Mary Oliver. Reprinted by permission of Beacon Press.

Index of Titles and First Lines

Titles are in *italics*.

ALSO AVAILABLE

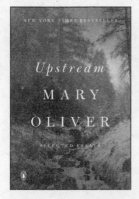

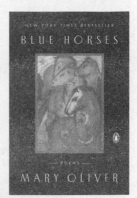

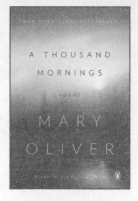